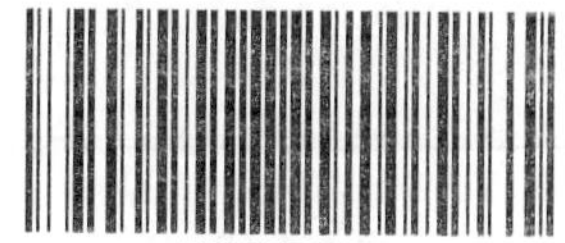

~SCHOONER "INTEGRITY"~

WALDO HOWLAND ~ OWNER

BUILT CONCORDIA YARD ~ SO. DARTMOUTH
MASSACHUSETTS ~ 1981 - 1982

R. D. CULLER ~ MASTER SHIPWRIGHT

LENGTH ~ 52' 0" B.P.
BEAM ~ 14' 8" MOULDED
DRAFT ~ 6' 3" (44' W.L.)
DISPLACEMENT ~ 29.5 LONG TONS

SCALE: 3/8" = 1'-0"

FISHERMAN

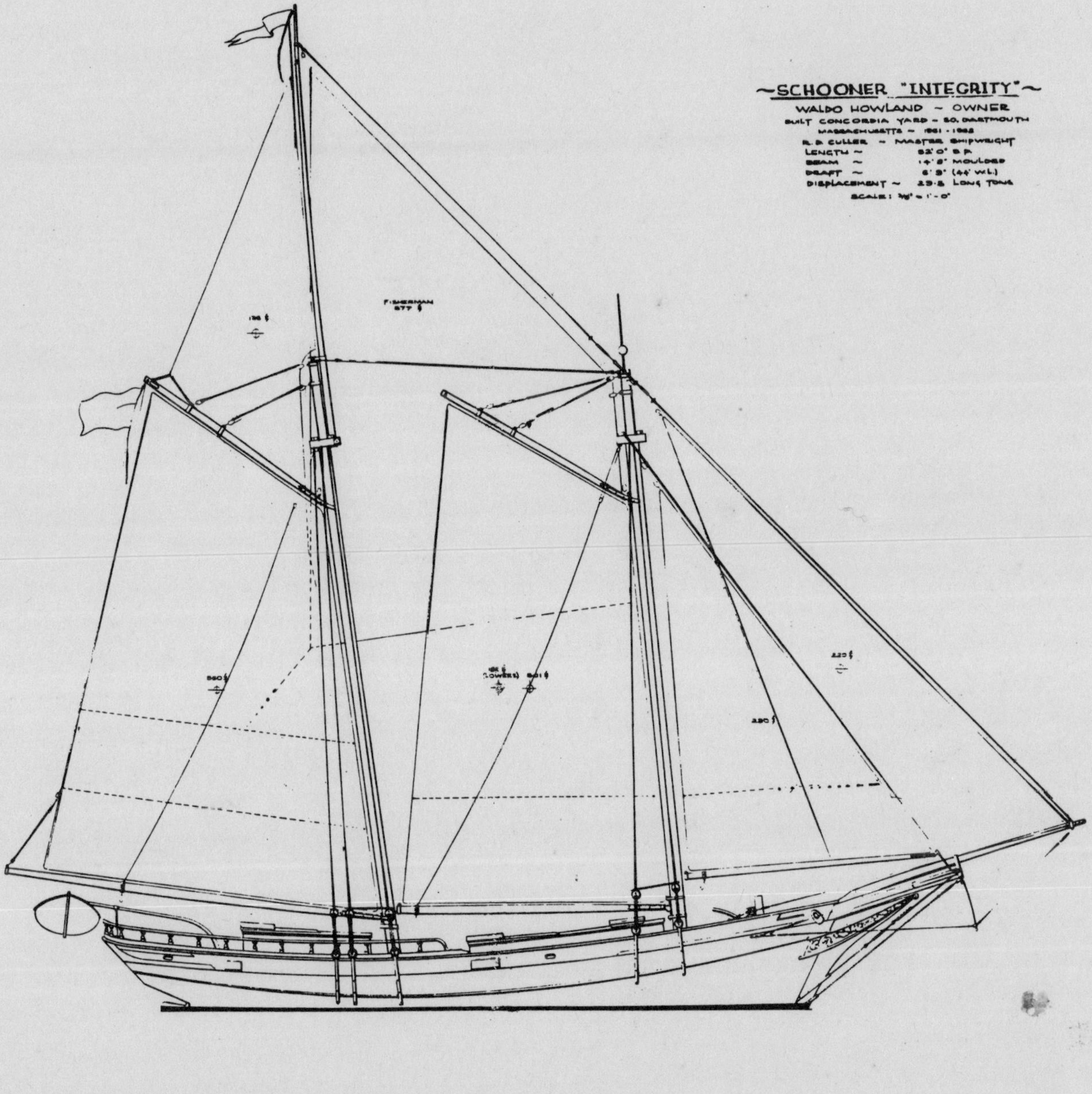

Integrity

A Life in Boats

Volume 3

A Life

Integrity IN BOATS

Waldo Howland

Mystic Seaport
75 Greenmanville Ave., PO Box 6000
Mystic, CT 06355-0990

Manufactured in the United States of America

Designed by Linda Cusano

ISBN 0-939510-86-3

To the memory of my mother,
Hope Waldo Howland
1877-1940

Contents

Part I ***Integrity***

1 A Reverence for Wood and Granite / **11**

2 Uncle Tod / **27**

3 Building *Integrity* / **43**

4 Chartering *Integrity* / **79**

Part II **Mystic Seaport**

5 Starting Out at Mystic Seaport / **115**

6 Tall Trees and Ship Timber / **131**

7 Refloating the *Charles W. Morgan* / **139**

8 A New Wharf for an Old Ship / **147**

9 Rebuilding the *Charles W. Morgan* / **155**

10 Building the Bulkheads / **165**

11 Yachting History and Mystic Seaport / **171**

12 Always Back to Boats / **179**

Index / **187**

Part I:
Integrity

The schooner *Integrity* visits Mystic Seaport in 1964.
(Mystic Seaport 1964-7-27-E)

1
A Reverence for Wood and Granite

I was born in Boston in 1908. But I have always considered myself a native of South Dartmouth, the town in southeastern Massachusetts where I spent the first (and most of the next 88) summers of my life. Indeed, my parents' address in South Dartmouth, 55 High Street, is still my street address some nine decades later. From High Street it is just a five-minute walk downhill to Padanaram Village and its excellent and historic little harbor.

I am not the only Howland to have chosen South Dartmouth as the place to live and work and enjoy my being. The first Howland to settle in these parts was my forebear Gideon Howland in the mid-1660s. Eleven generations and literally thousands of Gideon's descendants have made Dartmouth their home, right up to and including my own grandchildren. But in spite of being bound to this area by ties of blood and sentiment, the Howlands have often enough ventured to faraway places, especially by sea. Many have earned their living from the sea, from fishing and whaling in the 18th and 19th centuries to yacht building in my own case. Even when they have not, the Howlands' affinity for the sea and sailing has persisted.

The exterior of my parents' house in Padanaram was of handsome Colonial Revival design, but was built out of an experimental pinkish terra cotta tile that my father, then working for Waldo Brothers in the building materials business in Boston, was seeking to promote. The tile was not especially well-suited to the climate of our coast. On the other hand, it had a warm and pleasing color, not to mention being highly distinctive.

As for the interior of the house, that harkened back to the golden years

My parents' summer house at 55 High Street, South Dartmouth, viewed from the west. Built of terra cotta tile blocks in 1908, when my father was in the building materials business, the house was dismantled several years after his death in 1954. In its place my son Charlie built a wooden house with a gambrel roof that follows the general shape of the original Barnabas Howland house at Round Hill. Unidentified photographer (Author's collection)

of Old Dartmouth and New Bedford, when the whaling industry brought great wealth to New Bedford's whaling merchants and made the city one of the richest communities in America. Although the Howland whaling fortune had vanished by the time my father came of age, our Padanaram house was full of relics from those days of glory.

Right inside the cypress front door was a primitive sketch in color of the whaleship *George and Susan*, which was named after my great-great-grandfather George Howland and his second wife. It is attributed to a cabin boy on the vessel who executed it during a whaling voyage. I now know that the ship herself was built on the shore of Padanaram Harbor just a few hundred yards from the eventual location of South Wharf and my boat yard, Concordia Company.

Further into the front hall stood a massive chest made by a great friend of my grandfather William D. Howland, Arthur Grinnell–Uncle Arthur, as

A view of the southwest corner of the living room at 55 High Street, South Dartmouth, shortly after my father's death in 1954. The whaling print over the mantel is by Guarneray. The oil painting over the large table lamp is by William Bradford. Photograph by Samuel B. Potter. (Author's collection)

we were taught to call him. It was made from oak salvaged from the Howland whaleship *Rousseau* (pronounced "Russo," so as not to seem to endorse the philosophy of Jean-Jacques Rousseau, for whom the vessel had originally been built and named in 1802 by its first owner, the Philadelphia merchant Stephen Girard). The top of the chest featured finely carved panels of whaling scenes. Inside, carved letters affirmed that the chest had been a gift from Uncle Arthur to his friend Dillwyn Howland.

Also in the hall was a finely rigged model of a whaleship with decks, rails, houses, and whaleboats all perfectly reproduced. My father later gave this masterpiece to his longtime friend Allan Forbes, then president of Boston's State Street Trust Company. Last time I saw her, she sailed in grandeur over a teller's window.

Primitive watercolor of whaleship *George and Susan* believed to have been painted by Alexander Howland. Formerly owned by Llewellyn Howland. According to the legend on the verso of this watercolor, "Ship *George & Susan* [was] named by Geo. Howland, owner. She was built at Dartmouth, Mass. in 1810 and commissioned on the Howlands' wedding day. This ship returned from a voyage July 12, 1845 in command of Capt. [Alexander] Howland, who was once a cabin-boat on this same ship and painted this picture. Vessel was altered to a bark 1865. Last voyage 1877." (Courtesy of the New Bedford Whaling Museum-Old Dartmouth Historical Society)

Elsewhere in the Padanaram house were countless reminders of whaling days: prints, paintings, scrimshaw, harpoons, and more. Even Mother's garden had a whaling motif: two large cast-iron trypots that had formerly been used for trying out whale blubber were filled with soil and flowers in season.

Now that I am myself old, I wish more than ever that I had talked more with Mother and Father about family possessions and family history. As it is, I know all too little, and those who could have answered my questions are dead and gone. Although good libraries and museums are able to help in many instances, the ultimate resource for most of us is the memory of the old folks. And this is one of the reasons I am trying now to set down a little first-hand information that may prove useful to those who follow me.

From my own family, it is not much of a step to that larger family that I have cherished throughout my life: the men and women, old and young, who sail boats for pleasure, and those of us who have, as well, earned our living from the sea. I am grateful indeed that Mystic Seaport should have encouraged and helped so much with the two earlier volumes in this sailing autobiography. The experience has convinced me that firsthand accounts such as these, undramatic and ordinary though they may be, become in a few

"The very end of America's whaling era passed before my eyes. . . ." The bark *Charles W. Morgan*, homeward bound on her final whaling voyage, July 1921. Photographed off New Bedford by Dr. Henry D. Prescott. (Courtesy of New Bedford Whaling Museum-Old Dartmouth Historical Society)

Aerial view of *Charles W. Morgan* enshrined in her coffer dam at Round Hill, South Dartmouth, about 1930. Col. E.H.R. Green's airfield and blimp hangar (complete with blimp) are clearly visible at upper left. Photograph by Bert Hill, a skilled pilot and long the man in charge of operations at the Round Hill estate. (Courtesy of Roberta H. Sawyer)

Rerigged as a ship and dressed with the house flags of New Bedford whaling agents, the *Charles W. Morgan* is dedicated as a museum ship at her berth at Round Hill in 1925. The giant sand box in which she is incased was built of wooden sheathing and pilings held in place with solid rocks on the north and east sides, stone riprap on the south and west sides. Photograph by Albert Cook Church. (Mystic Seaport, 1960.453)

years an integral part of the written record of our past. Maritime history in all its many forms is what Mystic Seaport is all about. I am proud to be able to contribute to the Museum this final chapter in my own maritime history.

One summer day as I stood on Ricketson's Beach in Padanaram gazing south across Buzzards Bay, I saw the very end of America's whaling era pass before my eyes. A strange and wondrous ship was sailing silently in toward New Bedford Harbor, her working sails drawing well before a light but favorable breeze. Although I did not realize it at the time, this was the whaleship *Charles W. Morgan* coming home from her last whaling voyage. A host of such whalers had returned to New Bedford in years and decades gone by, but less than a handful would follow in the *Morgan*'s wake.

View of the forecastle of Bark *Charles W. Morgan*, ca. 1922 or later. Photograph by J.S. Martin. (Courtesy of New Bedford Whaling Museum-Old Dartmouth Historical Society)

This happened in 1921. At the time I was still a schoolboy and spent most of each year as a boarding student at Milton Academy in Milton, Massachusetts. My summers were my own, however, and I was to see more of the *Morgan* during succeeding years. First the *Morgan* was tied up at the foot of Union Street in New Bedford. Father took me down there several times to see her, and what I remember most from those visits was her smell–nothing really bad, but, especially when I went below, a strange new atmosphere. Not long after this, the *Morgan* gained national attention for her role in the motion picture *Down to the Sea in Ships*. Much of the movie was filmed on her decks and down below. Clara Bow made her film debut in her role as a tomboy, but many New Bedford and Padanaram people had bit parts in the movie, including my older sister Priscilla.

Then in 1924 the island steamer *Sankaty* caught fire at her berth in New Bedford. There was big excitement when she broke loose and drifted over to Fairhaven, where the *Morgan* was now berthed. The *Sankaty* gave the *Morgan* a scorching before the Fairhaven fire department got things under control.

Although I don't recall taking any special interest in the *Morgan* during those years, I did feel sorry that she was in such shabby condition. I also knew that

Harry Neyland, a marine artist and close neighbor of ours, was trying along with others to raise money to save and preserve her for a New Bedford museum. Neyland had no luck with these efforts until he approached Colonel Edward Howland Robinson Green, son of Hetty Green, "the Witch of Wall Street." Colonel Green's grandfather Edward Mott Robinson had owned the *Morgan* for a time. The Colonel agreed to help get the old ship back into good shape, buy her new sails, and maintain her at the Round Hill property he had inherited from his (and my) Howland ancestors. For this project he hired Captain George Fred Tilton to supervise repairs and to prepare a waterfront berth on the South Beach at Round Hill at which to display her.

I wish that I had watched the building of the cofferdam that was created for the *Morgan*. As it is, I can only guess that they built three sides of a stone box off the beach, then by some dredging floated the *Morgan* into it, built the outer–or fourth–side, and, as a final step, filled the completed coffer (or box or coffin) with sand and gravel to hold the ship steady.

The *Morgan* took to her new berth at Round Hill in the spring of 1925. This was the same spring when I became the half-owner of a late-1923 Model T Ford, which allowed me to make frequent visits to Round Hill. Colonel Green allowed my friends and me to come in and enjoy broadcasts from his outdoor radio speakers, his swimming pool with the high-diving board, the activity on his private airstrip, and the run of the *Morgan* under the supervision of Captain Tilton. Round Hill was a delightful place to be, and the *Morgan* looked grand and happy there.

In 1930 an organization called Whaling Enshrined took over direction of the *Morgan*. I have listed in an appendix the names of those involved in Whaling Enshrined because they were all prominent citizens of the New Bedford area. If any local group could have taken care of the last New Bedford whaleship, these men could and probably should have.

After I graduated from Harvard in 1930, I didn't see much of the *Morgan*. But as the lean years of the Great Depression went on, I began to feel more and more sorry for her. First Captain Tilton died in 1932, then Colonel Green died three years later, leaving no money in his will for the *Morgan*'s maintenance. This was strike one. Strike two was the 1938 hurricane, which caused severe damage to the *Morgan*. Strike three came when efforts failed to raise any appreciable amount of local money for a *Morgan* museum in New Bedford. In 1940 things could hardly have looked worse for the *Morgan*–or the world as a whole.

The hurricane of 1938 that damaged the *Charles W. Morgan* completely destroyed *Escape*, the 40-foot Norwegian pilot boat that Father and I owned and sailed with such pleasure (see volume one, *A Life in Boats: The Years Before the War*).

Waldo and Katy Howland, 1941. Photograph by the author. (Author's collection)

Indeed, when the storm drove *Escape* against the stone causeway that forms the westerly end of the Padanaram Bridge, the grand old boat literally split in two. Her starboard half was ground to pieces; but her port half remained largely intact, even to dishes and glasses unbroken in the pantry locker.

There was much gear aboard *Escape* that could be salvaged, but we had to get about it quickly before the "heartless people" beat us to it. I especially remember one rogue approaching me as I was rescuing the cabin lamp. "Leave that alone," he shouted, "I picked that out for myself." And I said, "It's my boat and my lamp, and I bet you throw stones at your mother." He may not have gotten my point, but, at any rate, I saved the lamp.

We collected and trucked an appreciable assortment of *Escape*'s equipment up to Father's house, where I as a young bachelor was then living. Since we had no suitable place to store it, we decided then and there to build a boat shed. As with so many good ideas, the shed project expanded every time my parents or I thought about it. Step by step the concept evolved from simple storage shed to mansion of happiness.

When we finally decided to go forward with construction, our first move was to climb over the boundary stone wall and consult with our nearest neighbor, Wilton Gifford. Mr. Gifford, a retired contractor, was a first-class carpenter and a wonderful man. Sixty-five cents an hour was his standing rate. His father had sailed a whaling voyage or two out of New Bedford as a ship's carpenter. His mother had sold my parents the land on which we lived then and on which I and some of my children live now. He had a shop, simply but well equipped, in the rear of his house and some very sound and helpful ideas in the back of his head. Both his shop and his ideas he shared with the Howlands most generously.

Mr. Gifford gave every job his careful consideration and then tackled it in his sound and deliberate way. At the end of each day he had accomplished

Waldo Howland's house on High Street, South Dartmouth. The house was originally built in 1941-42, as an extension of the existing high stone wall. It has since been expanded in several stages. Hope Howland's pear orchard and garden flourished in the lee of the wall. Photograph by author. (Author's collection)

wonders. I can remember so well his strong right arm going up and down in slow, steady strokes as his saw walked its way accurately through his drawn line. From him I learned that machine tools are not necessary for many jobs. The right hand-tools, kept sharp, often save time in the end. And I can't help but think of Mr. Gifford when I see a shipyard carpenter climb up out of his job, walk across the shop to the table saw, adjust the blade, cut his board, then return to his work, only to find that his measurements are slightly off and many minutes already gone forever.

A clean piece of wrapping paper, a pencil and rule, and Mr. Gifford's straight-forward approach were all that were needed to develop the shed building plans. Thirty feet was length enough for small spars; 18 feet was width enough to allow for good storage space and for a span not too wide for rafters and cellar beams of modest dimensions. Height was settled for us, as you will shortly see. And the pitch of the simple gable roof was eight inches up for every twelve inches along. This was the rule of thumb for Cape Cod cottages and white cedar shingles. A greater pitch was a waste of material; a lesser one was an invitation to hold snow or cause leaks. And besides being right, the pitch looks right.

Originally, the floor was to be dirt only. But then Mother decided that a cellar ventilated by area-way pipe at one end and by a chimney flue in the middle would make a good and much needed root cellar for her garden crops. She was quite right; we can keep Hubbard squash until March in the space beneath what has become our living-room floor.

Mr. Gifford believed in local materials and, in general, so do I. Indigenous materials used with understanding serve their purposes well and they fit comfortably with their surroundings. It was Mother who suggested that we use local stone for the walls, and this was no idle whim. Some years before, she had designed, and had had her gardener Charlie Ponte build, an eight-foot-high stone wall to protect from cold spring breezes a double row of pear trees that bordered, and in summer shaded, her garden path. A section of this wall would serve as the east wall of our building (thereby dictating the height of the studs) and would snuggle neatly into the existing plantings.

Charlie Ponte came to America the same year I did, only I arrived via home delivery at 54 Burroughs Street, Jamaica Plain, Massachusetts, and he came, by then a young man, along with a case of smallpox and on a small, crowded packet schooner from St. Vincent, one of the Cape Verde islands. In fact, many Cape Verdeans had earlier reached New Bedford aboard whaling vessels. But Charlie was one of a second wave of immigrants. He came at a time when New Bedford mill owners were flooding Cape Verde with propaganda leaflets illustrated with pictures of bags of gold. Fortunately for Charlie and the Howlands, he never worked in a mill; for he was a gardener at heart and in spirit. A citizen he never became, but he stayed with our family all his working life. He grew beautiful and lasting hedges of box, yew, privet, and arbor vitae; he raised vegetables wonderful to eat; and he built fine stone walls. I want to believe he enjoyed his work. I know that my family and I continue to enjoy the results of it.

The decision to use stone for the walls of the shed turned out to be a fortuitous one, because it prompted Mr. Gifford to call in his Westport friend Elmer Pierce to help with the project. Elmer was a stone mason. Once to know him was always to remember him (and his 16-cylinder Cadillac touring car) with admiration, affection, and joy.

Granite is a durable wall material, and in order to provide long-lived frame stock to go with it, Elmer recommended that we use locust. He assured me then, and I assure you now, that locust would last one year longer than stone. So our sills, plates, floor joists, cellar beams, and window and door frames are all of locust. After 58 years, they are still as sound and almost as hard as the granite walls.

Locust doesn't grow in lumber yards. It seems to grow in small groves and special, sometimes out-of-the-way areas. It is not confined to New England, but is found throughout the United States, as well as in Europe and elsewhere. I am told that it is one of the first trees to take hold again after a bad fire or environmental calamity. As luck would have it, Father's boatman

Martin Jackson was living in Bristol, Rhode Island, about the time we were building the shed. He reported that one of the hay fields in Bristol was surrounded with locust trees. Nicely spaced from each other (having apparently rooted from green locust fence posts), the Bristol locusts were straight and sound, with no sign of the ants that sometimes infest locusts. It was, to be sure, very sad that the 1938 hurricane had blown down so many of the trees. It was sad, too, that in their fallen position they hampered the operations of the farmer who

Living room at Padanaram facing north, 1955. The banjo clock over the left side of the mantlepiece was made by Sherman Fearing for Hope Waldo Howland. The oil painting is of Cuttyhunk and was a wedding present to Waldo and Katy Howland from the artist, Clifford W. Ashley. The side chairs and rocking chair were made by John Waldo, the author's uncle. The small English brick of the fireplace were from Clifford Ashley's house in New Bedford. The walls and overhead are pine; the counter and sink black walnut (as is the floor); the collar beams are locust. Photograph by Norman Fortier. (Author's collection)

The living room of Waldo Howland's house at Padanaram showing big recessed windows open to south and west, 1955. Photograph by Norman Fortier. (Author's collection)

owned them. The situation had its positive side for the Howlands, however. With considerable effort, much groaning of truck springs, but some pleasure, too, we cut and trucked the locusts to the sawmill in Russell's Mills, Dartmouth.

This water-powered mill was run by Mr. Sheehan. He had been in the sawing and grinding business for many years, and he knew the difficulties of sawing locusts. Still, he cheerfully undertook our project, insisting only that we pay for any saw teeth damaged by hidden nails. The locust did not break any saw teeth, but it definitely dulled a few before the job was done.

Good stone walls take time to build. For every hour of Elmer's time, however, I gained an hour's worth of beautiful wall and an hour's education and pleasure. And on Sunday mornings, when his wife and other good folks were learning important things in church, Elmer and I were traveling around the Westport countryside discussing how important things used to be done–and lining up special stones for the house. A good, flat fieldstone with several good faces or one that had already served as a capstone on some ancient pasture wall: these were the ones we looked for. The cost of the stones was paid partially in coin, but also in long conversations about the weather, the state of the crops, and the history of Westport, about which Elmer knew a great deal.

In actual building, Elmer faced up the outside of the house walls with flat stones of the best appearance that he fitted closely together so as to require

Photographed by the author in 1943, the house has already been expanded with its first wood-frame addition on the northwest corner. The yew hedge still screens the house from High Street traffic 60 years later. (Author's collection)

the narrowest of cement seams. He did the inside face equally well, but with less attention to appearance. The space between he filled with irregular small stones and chips that would best tie the structure together. And what a beautiful job he did with the window openings, their side faces made of lichen-covered capstones flaring generously inward! The low windowsills on the south and west sides of the house he fashioned from slabs of silver stone that once formed a sunny sidewalk in New Bedford. Two high window openings and one low one Elmer chipped out of Charlie Ponte's garden wall to form the windows on the east side. The door openings were not flared, but they too were carefully faced to accept the locust door frames.

Some people say that work of this quality and integrity is no longer practical. In today's strange world, where no one stays put for more than a few years, perhaps they are right. Nonetheless, Elmer's stone walls have served their purpose well. No one has since wearied his hand or raided his pocketbook to repair or treat them in any way. The walls have paid their way many times over, and this is good and comforting to think about.

While the stonework was taking shape, Mr. Gifford took me east a few miles to Hartley's sawmill in Rochester. We were on the hunt for good native pine, and this was Mr. Hartley's stock in trade. He sold us what we needed for roof and interior joinerwork at the price of three and a half cents a board foot, delivered. The pine had been cut locally in the late fall, when the sap was down. It had been sawed during the winter and then "stuck" outside to air-dry in February snows and March winds. One pine log, some 16 feet long by 30 inches in diameter through the butt, lay by itself unsawn in the mill yard. My curiosity and ignorance prompted me to ask why. Mr. Hartley told me that circular saws of the sort used by local mills were some four feet in diameter and thus limited to turning out lumber some 22 inches in width or less. Mr. Hartley was willing to spend a bit of extra time to worry off a slab of that noble log, lay the side thus flattened on the mill carriage, and then proceed with sawing out one-inch boards 22 inches wide and mostly of heartwood. I have never regretted paying five cents a board foot for those great planks of clear pine, nor do I mind in the least looking at them daily as I eat my eggs and toast in our kitchen room.

Wood, like a friend, is better company and more useful if you understand it and treat it well. Pine is a small word, but it covers many variations of trees. Our pine is more generally known as Eastern White Pine and grows from northern New England down to the Carolinas and west to the Great Lakes. It seems to be more durable if grown within 75 miles or so of salt water. Perhaps the salt air pickles it as it grows. Older trees (often called virgin pine) seem to be of better quality and more resistant to rot. Since only the bark and sapwood in a tree is really alive, the center of a 200-year-old tree has been seasoning for a long time.

Pine likes to grow in hollows behind ridges, as it does in the back areas of Plymouth and Carver, and in Rochester and Lakeville. In this way it does not get battered and weakened by gales. It likes to rest under a blanket of snow in winter and to drink during thaws in spring.

On and on it goes, and I wish I knew more about pine's secrets. I do know that the New England colonies went to war with England partly because His Royal Majesty marked and took away our best pine trees, especially in the Piscataqua area of New Hampshire. These were made into spars for the Royal Navy, which tolerated nothing but the best. I myself have seen and can still find New England sheds built 75 and more years ago that were sided with pine boards set vertically. These boards have never been covered or treated in any way, but still remain sound and silvery beautiful. Pine, or any wood that is used horizontally, for that matter, such as clapboards, will not stand the weather as well as it does when used vertically. Instead of running off, water tends to get trapped and cause rot. I have taken 30-year-old shingles off an old house and applied them to the sides of a new building. Thin they were from the wear of many rains, but they were otherwise entirely serviceable.

Great-grandfather George Howland always admonished his captains to "be kind to the crew" and to "salt the mastheads." The lower masts of New Bedford whaleships were native pine; they often outlasted one ship and were then transferred to another one. Did you ever notice that some old hospitals and schoolhouses were located in pine groves? Pine groves must have a therapeutic quality. At least they sing a lovely song in a gentle breeze and waft a lovely smell in the warm summer sun.

Yes, Rochester Mahogany, as some natives call it, is my favorite wood. It must never be confused with those pines that grow in the western part of the United States. The Western White, the Sugar, the Ponderosa, and others do grow taller and bigger than ours, are often freer of knots, and have other commercial values, but they can't be trusted to stand the onslaughts of wind and weather, nor as furniture do they smile in the same sunny way, at least in my opinion.

Mr. Gifford and his carpenter friend Mr. Rogers had framed up our house and put the roof on, and they were shingling when Mr. Gifford suddenly and unexpectedly died of a heart attack. Before she joined her life's companion not long after, Mrs. Gifford did two things that have affected my existence ever since. First, she offered me Mr. Gifford's tool shop, which I did use for a time and from which I still have some of the tools. I am glad, however, that I never moved the shop itself from the Gifford's property to my own, because this little building has been a most productive and happy center for our neighbors' children and grandchildren, and for ours as well. I'm not against playing ping pong in the church basement, mind you, but I am strongly in favor of young people learning to make real things out of wood.

The second blessing that Mrs. Gifford bestowed was an introduction to her carpenter nephew, Ben Tripp. Ben built my brother's house in 1941 and worked with the Howlands for many years until he left to become building inspector for the Town of Dartmouth.

After the death of Wilton Gifford, I asked Elmer Pierce what we were going to do now. I remember Elmer rolling his eyes heavenward and then saying, "Well, I have another basket of tools. I'll bring it over and we'll see about finishing up the carpentry on your house." And that, with Mr. Rogers's cooperation, he proceeded to do, tackling the whole job with carefully executed joints that required few if any moldings, just the way a good stone mason joins his stones. The result was unusual woodwork of unique appeal and finish, not unlike the character of Elmer Pierce himself.

And what, you may ask, became of the salvaged pieces and equipment from the old *Escape*? We used some of it in the house, including a piece of her deck in our entryway and some of the specially fitted cast-iron ballast in our fireplace. Much of the spars and rigging went into the ketch *Prospector*, whose construction I was overseeing at the time (see volume one, *A Life in Boats: The Years Before the War*). As for the house itself, it has since had four additions (of wood, not stone) to make room for my five children. As of this writing, three of my children surround the original house with houses and children of their own.

2
Uncle Tod

The 55-foot schooner *Integrity* was designed and built along the time-proven lines of the traditional small packet schooners that had such an important role in the development of our part of the world in the days of working sail. For ten years *Integrity* played a vital part in my life and in the life of my family. She continues to do so today in the form of happy and constructive memories.

I have always wanted to write about *Integrity*. But when, belatedly, I started on her story, I found it very hard to decide just where and how to begin. And so matters stood until I received a provocative letter from my friend Nicholas Whitman.

Nick and I began working together in 1978, when he was in charge of the photography department at the New Bedford Whaling Museum. Thanks to a very generous benefactor, we had the privilege and the satisfaction of helping the museum create a first-class facility for the conservation, preservation, and cataloging of its priceless collection of photographic negatives and images. More recently, as an independent photographer, Nick had gone through most of my own negatives and had put them in order, with contact prints as finding aids. Among the images were photographs of *Integrity* that had been taken during her construction, along with some views of her being commissioned and, later, under sail.

In his letter Nick wrote:

> After printing your last group of negatives I decided I had better reread *A Life in Boats* to learn a little about what I had been looking at.

Photographer Nick Whitman's Beetle Cat, around 1986. Whitman rebuilt the boat himself for use on the Westport River. Photograph by Nicholas Whitman. (Author's collection)

I went back to the period of *Flying Cloud* for starters, but then continued reading right through both volumes. There was so much that had gotten by me the first time–ideas, vessel designs, history, seamanship, business practices, personal biography, and, my favorite, the lessons you've gleaned from these various experiences–that it was as if I had not read the books before at all.

I am thrilled that a third volume is in the works. And I write you now because there are many ideas relevant to me personally that you have not already addressed. One obvious question is why your dream boat, *Integrity*, was modeled after a coasting schooner. Whether by Bill Harris or Ray Hunt, Concordia's designs were so progressive that they are now at once classics and yet not dated at all. Why look so far back for a design? And if a schooner it had to be, why not a Bill Hand design of the *Flying Cloud* type? Why choose a workboat for a model? And how about taking a design and scaling it down for you purpose? Can't that be troublesome?

Don't get me wrong, I'm not questioning your decision. But I'd be interested to learn how you came to it and, of course, how it turned out.

It seems to me that your ideas have proven to be at once conservative and prophetic. Take for example your decision to continue building wooden Beetle Cat boats in the face of the fiberglass revolution. The Beetle Cat endures, and since the building of *Integrity* a renaissance in wood boatbuilding and appreciation has occurred. I knew that Peter Culler designed *Integrity*, but having just read his design catalogue I discover that you and Concordia Company are mentioned more than anyone else. What about Pete Culler and his boats? He sure looked back to look ahead.

Nick's question about why I chose a coasting schooner as a model for my own boat startled me at first because, actually, I didn't have a ready answer to it. I knew I was glad that I had made the decision. And I knew that owning *Integrity* had not merely been a wonderful experience on its own terms, but that it had led me ever so surely to a second career with boats at Mystic Seaport. Nevertheless, the thinking behind *Integrity* may deserve some careful analysis. For as Nick Whitman has suggested, she does at first glance appear quite different from any boat that Concordia had designed or built previously.

The line between pleasure and work boat is not always easy to draw, and a bit of well-tended brightwork or a gilded cove stripe sometimes is enough to transform the latter to the former. Admitting that Concordia had traditionally specialized in yachts, I would say that many of the boats I dealt with did definitely hark back to traditional workboat designs–designs that had over many years proved their suitability for the job they had to do.

For example, the Beetle Cats that Concordia built are a smaller version of the workboats that before the days of the internal combustion engine (and for some time after) were used by fishermen and lobstermen and for general 'longshore work in New England waters and elsewhere. As the pioneering English yacht designer and writer Dixon Kemp wrote in his *Manual of Yachts and Small Craft*, the catboat will "always be popular as a harbor craft."

The Concordia 31 sloops are another popular class that go back, at least in spirit, to the construction and utilitarian finish of earlier workboats. Simple wood construction has its own charm and functional appeal. Designed by Concordia's Wilder B. (Bill) Harris with economy in mind, the Concordia 31s are smart sailers and comfortable cruisers.

The ketch *Prospector* was designed by Bill Harris as the mobile home base for a prospector looking for gold in South America. She was intended to be economical to build, maintain, and operate, and her general shape and rig were distinctly influenced by the practices and forms of working vessels, in particular England's Brixham trawlers.

The Concordia-designed ketch *Prospector* on her first sailing trials off Fort Lauderdale, Florida, 1941. Built by John M. Harper, Jr., for Neil W. Rice of Manchester, Massachusetts, *Prospector* measured 42'7" overall (38'6" on the waterline), with a 12'6" beam and 6' draft. The photograph was taken by Pete Culler from the deck of his self-built replica of Captain Joshua Slocum's *Spray*. (Author's collection)

I understand that the philosophy of pleasure-boat design has changed since the advent of gas and diesel engines, the forty-hour week, and the new emphasis on high-speed performance and minimal maintenance. I accept the fact there are now and always will and should be many serious sailors who will actively pursue the latest trends. But my own tendency is increasingly to look back and to consider the tried and true–and not to be led away too quickly or too far by the untried and the untested. I am sure this accounts for my current deep interest in the work of Mystic Seaport, which has done so well preserving worthy examples of our maritime past: the actual boats where that is possible; the artifacts, documents, and records where it is not. I have the strong feeling that those of us interested in the sea and ships should always find time to look back as well as forward. The sea and the winds do not change, and some boats reflect this fact and some do not, to the pleasure or sorrow of those who sail them.

Nick Whitman's letter challenged me not only to reflect on the boats and the history that had influenced my decision to build *Integrity*, but further to acquaint my readers with three of the seamen who so greatly helped me in choosing the model for my family ship.

The first of these mentors was Rodman Swift. This delightful man was my father's contemporary and lifelong friend. They both came from New Bedford seafaring families that had lived by the waters of Buzzards Bay since the mid-17th century. They had both inherited a love of sailing and of the ways of the sea. In different ways they both left lasting impressions on the boating world.

Generations of the Swift family had been New Bedford merchants involved in the business of outfitting ships. One of their specialties had been dealing in live oak and hard pine lumber for sale to New Bedford shipbuilders, and this had compelled some members of the family to spend several months each year in the Carolinas, Georgia, and Florida collecting lumber for shipment north. The outfitting business flourished until the Civil War. Thereafter, much of the remaining whaling industry moved out to the Pacific and Arctic and was serviced primarily by outfitters in San Francisco and Hawaii.

Rodman Swift's father, Frederick, married Sarah Rotch, daughter of William J. and Emily (Morgan) Rotch. The Rotch family had had a primary role in bringing the whaling business to New Bedford and thereby transforming New Bedford from a small village to a wealthy city. Sarah Rotch was also descended from two other dominant whaling families, the Morgans and the Rodmans.

The Frederick Swifts had a winter house on the corner of Arnold and Orchard Streets in New Bedford. They also had a big summer cottage in Nonquitt, a private waterfront colony located near Round Hill in South Dartmouth, where the whaleship *Charles W. Morgan* was enshrined before World War II. Nonquitt overlooks a cove that is protected from all but punishing southeast storms. Its beach front is terminated on the north by the old stone post office wharf and on the south by a granite ledge that is topped by a huge boulder. Between these two landmarks are two beaches. The northerly beach is perfect for the landing and tethering of skiffs; the southerly one is a crescent of gently sloping soft sand that is perfect for swimming.

It was here in Nonquitt that Rodman Swift got his start in boating. Father told me that Rodman's first boat was a five-foot punt–definitely a singlehander. A punt, by the way, is a flat-bottomed craft like a skiff, except that it is squared off at the bow as well as the stern, allowing for greater full-length stability. In such a sound and maneuverable little boat any youngster who has a mind to can learn basic seafaring skills that will automatically stay with him and reward him ever after. For whatever reason, boating lessons learned firsthand and early on stick with one more faithfully than does knowledge acquired later on in life.

Rodman soon graduated into a larger boat. This was *Jag*, a 16-foot open, round-bottomed fishing boat of well-proven design. As I visualize *Jag*, she is something like the Culler-designed sloop boats we built at Concordia, although she had no deck or shelter of any sort and was rigged with two

The Concordia Sloop Boat

Inspired by such working craft as the Kingston lobster boat, Connecticut River shad boat, and Bahamas sailing dinghy, the Concordia sloop boat was designed by Waldo Howland and Pete Culler and built by the Concordia Company. Her dimensions of 17'8" overall, 16'5" on the waterline, with a 5' beam and 1'6" draft with the center-board up) make her a comfortable boat to handle with a sail area of 166 square feet in her classic gaff-rigged main and jib. Besides her centerboard, lead ballast gives her stability.

A Concordia Company brochure described her attributes. "Like her older sisters, our sloop is handy and maneuver-able. She holds her course and does not rely on constant use of the rudder. At anchor she lays quietly head to wind with mainsail set. She is sufficiently heavy and of such design that she carries her way well. Shooting a mooring or coming alongside another vessel or float can be accom-plished without haste or confusion. There are no shrouds, and as both boom and gaff have jaws it is possible to sail by the lee or lay alongside with wind abaft the beam."

Here a Concordia sloop boat reaches across Padanaram Harbor, with Kin Howland at the helm and Susie and Waldo Howland Jr., (and spaniel Bill) as crew. Photograph by Norman Fortier. (Courtesy of the photog-rapher)

masts fitted with spritsails. In this smack boat, as Father called her, Rodman ventured well beyond the confines of the harbor, out into Buzzards Bay and across to the Elizabeth Islands and Martha's Vineyard. His trips in *Jag* were often real cruises that lasted a week, or until his food supply ran low.

It was aboard *Jag* that Rodman first mastered the arts and tasted the pleasures of the cruising life. Sailing sometimes with his older sister, Helen, and often by himself, he learned what equipment and supplies were essential and what could be left behind. Most important, he came to know and understand his boat and what the two of them together could and could not do. He learned to enjoy the sea by working with it and its ways, rather than by trying to confront it to suit a landsman's approach.

Like my father, Rodman began his school years in New Bedford at Friends Academy, then moved on to boarding school at Milton Academy. He attended Harvard College, from which he graduated in 1904 with a degree in mining engineering. During school and college summers he found himself in great demand as a crew aboard many different yachts.

In April 1905, just out of college, Rodman gave in to an irresistible urge to go to sea. He had hoped to sail aboard one of his New Bedford uncle Frank Stone's ships. Failing that, he shipped before the mast on the *Astral*, a bark belonging to the Standard Oil Company. The *Astral* was bound out from New York to Japan with a load of case oil (kerosene in cases), and this voyage lasted a year and carried him southeast around the Cape of Good Hope to Japan, then back across the Pacific Ocean to California. The voyage was a real seagoing experience the likes of which no other friends of mine have ever had. Rodman never talked too much about it, but on a later boat of his own he mounted on the cabin bulkhead a photograph that had been taken aloft in the *Astral* during a wicked storm that he would never forget. (For more on *Astral* and Captain Swift, see William H. Bunting's book *Sea Struck*, Gardiner, Maine, 2004.)

With this voyage under his belt, Rodman took the train back to New Bedford. Through a college roommate he acquired an engineering job at the North Star Mine in Grass Valley, California, where he worked as a surveyor. There he met the manager's daughter, Elizabeth Foote, whom he fell in love with and married. He continued working at the mine until 1910, when he moved back east with his wife and first-born daughter, Agnes. I would later meet Agnes at Milton Academy, when we shared a Bunsen burner in the school's science laboratory.

For the next 20 years Rodman worked for the Submarine Signal Company in Boston, the firm from which Raytheon subsequently evolved. His job involved considerable shipboard duty, which he greatly enjoyed. Looking for a house in Greater Boston, Rodman consulted a government chart instead of a road map and thereby discovered an old commercial stone wharf for sale in nearby Hingham harbor. On the wharf he built Wharf House, and from here he commuted to work at first by train, later by Model T Ford. In his off-hours, he enjoyed boating with his family, which soon included another daughter, Sally. Although Rodman's wife was never a cruising enthusiast, she enjoyed day-sailing and encouraged her daughters to follow Rodman's example.

In the early 1920s Rodman bought some 50 acres of high land at Gay Head on Martha's Vineyard, overlooking Menemsha Pond, Vineyard Sound, and Buzzards Bay. Here in due course and with his own hands he built a fieldstone cabin that had a wonderful view, but few facilities. Alone or with his daughters, Rodman made good use of the camp in the years that followed.

Rodman retired from Submarine Signal in 1931. His wife Betty died in

Rodman Swift aboard his little schooner *Tyche*, ca. 1955. Named for the Greek goddess of good fortune, *Tyche* (and her master) enjoyed a fortunate life by working with the sea, instead of trying to change it to suit a land-dweller's convenience. Designed by Sam Crocker in John Alden's design office, *Tyche* was built at the Baker Yacht Basin in Quincy, Massachusetts, in 1922. Photograph by Norman Fortier, neg. 20894. (Courtesy of the photographer)

1940. During World War II, when he could not sail and his daughters were grown and on their own, he retired to his cabin on the Vineyard and became a valued citizen of the island, farming seriously until peace came to the world again.

My own first connection with Uncle Tod, as I learned to call Rodman Swift, came in the early 1920s, when he sailed his new little schooner, *Tyche*, into Padanaram waters and set a mooring in the outer harbor. (This, by the

Dan and Dave Cheever's Concordia 31 sloop *Mary Ellen*, Rodman "Uncle Tod" Swift's schooner *Tyche*, and *Integrity*'s beach boat *Java* in the basin at South Wharf, ca. 1965. Each boat has such traditional lines that such a scene could have been photographed a century ago. Photograph by Norman Fortier. (Courtesy of the photographer)

way, was in almost exactly the same spot where some 40 years later I set the mooring for my own schooner, *Integrity*.) Snugly located in the lee of the breakwater, *Tyche* would not have the harbor fleet drag down on her during a southeast storm. The location was also clear of harbor traffic and in a picturesque sanctuary just off Ricketson's Point, from which Uncle Tod could easily row ashore to the Ricketson dock.

I began cruising with Uncle Tod in the mid-1930s. Concordia's new brokerage business had just been established, and I was selling a small fleet of secondhand Fishers Island 31-footers and delivering them from Fishers Island Sound to Buzzards Bay. Father suggested that I invite Uncle Tod to help me with the delivery operation. This was the birth of a delightful and educational association with Uncle Tod that continued until his death.

It was during a delivery trip that I learned something about Uncle Tod's planning for *Tyche*. In 1922, he got in touch with his friend Sam Crocker, who at the time was working in John Alden's yacht design office in downtown Boston. Together they discussed all the special features that Uncle Tod had in mind for his schooner. Sam then drew up the lines and construction plans. As built, the 27-foot *Tyche* was one of the smallest cruising boats ever to be rigged as an offshore schooner. But Uncle Tod visualized doing much of his future sailing alone; he felt strongly that two short masts and three small sails would be better for him than one taller mast with a big mainsail and jib. As proof of the correctness of his decision, he cruised safely aboard *Tyche* for the better part of 35 years. Before World War II, *Tyche* sailed in New England waters, with home ports in Padanaram and Menemsha. But for two years after the war she followed the good example of migrating birds and slowly wended her way south through the Intracoastal Waterway to Melbourne on the east coast of Florida. Here she sailed at will on a beautiful stretch of the Indian River.

The living quarters aboard *Tyche* were good and practical for Uncle Tod alone or with one guest, but were not of a size that would be useful for my family of seven. However, *Tyche* possessed many features that I was to keep in mind in planning my bigger one. She had a good system for handling a heavy anchor. Her separate engine and tank room worked out especially well. Her arrangement for getting the dory aboard was not only good but unique. A short boom with jaws to fit the foremast and a Spanish burton to hang from its end allowed Uncle Tod to stand way over on the port side of *Tyche*'s deck and thus heel the ship over a bit. This allowed him to attach his hoisting tackle to the bridle on the dory and then hoist her above rail level. By shifting his weight to starboard he then brought *Tyche* back to level and automatically swung the dory in on deck where he wanted her. Although stern davits would be more practical for handling *Integrity*'s dinghy, I closely followed Uncle Tod's system of oiling pine decks and using wire rigging and galvanized fittings. His maintenance procedures worked out well on *Integrity*, as I will later explain.

After two winter trips south with *Tyche* and some warnings of heart trouble, Uncle Tod bought a raised-deck powerboat in 1951 and kept her in Florida for four years as his winter home. In late January 1955 I received a welcome letter from Uncle Tod. He was in Melbourne Harbor, anchor-bound, aboard his Old Man Winter boat, *Muskrat*. His doctor had forbidden him to do any cruising even in the protected waterway, unless he had a boating friend to go with him. His letter suggested that I must be badly in need of a ten-day vacation, before the spring rush began at Concordia.

So one fine morning in early February I stepped off the train at Melbourne. There was no waiting on the platform. Uncle Tod spotted me immediately, picked up my seabag, and led me to his 1941 Plymouth Coupe, an exact duplicate of my own in Padanaram. Soon we were parked in the shade of some trees set back a few feet from a small sandy beach. There, half pulled-out, lay Uncle Tod's tender, a beautifully shaped little flat-bottom skiff that had already safely carried its owners from one point to another for over 70 years.

It was a short pull to Uncle Tod's 35-foot *Muskrat*. While I was down below shifting to my boat shoes, Uncle Tod quietly hoisted his skiff aboard into its special place in the cockpit, using the boom and tackle rigged from *Muskrat*'s short mast. After Uncle Tod asked whether I was all set to go, he started up the engine and sent me forward to cast off the mooring line. On most boats this would have required me to step up and walk forward along a narrow deck, but on *Muskrat* all I had to do was walk through the cabin to the forward cockpit, from which anchor and mooring lines could be easily handled without getting up on deck at all. Returning aft I found my captain sitting at the wheel on a special cushion placed atop the bow of the skiff. The height of the seat was perfect. Vision was good in every direction, The cockpit shelter gave ample shade. And Uncle Tod had easy passage to any part of his ship.

I sat down alongside him on the starboard cockpit seat, and off down the Inland Waterway we slipped, passing Cape Malabar, Roseland, Wabasso, and Winter Beach, and coming finally to rest in an exquisite little anchorage just off the waterway. This was Snake Bird Cove, named after the Anhinga, the bird that fishes so beautifully underwater.

Here out of the traffic, with almost perfect privacy and in partial shade, we were enjoying a sandwich lunch, only to be interrupted when Uncle Tod caught sight of a little powerboat approaching the anchorage. He hustled me below, explaining: "That's Randy Clifford's boat, *Puffin*, and he'll be going fishing this afternoon and he will insist on giving us some of his catch. But I just don't want fish today. So we'll stay in our bunks for a spell until Randy and his wife go down for their naps. Then we can *escape* for the afternoon." In fact, this was just what I wanted, a little stretch out. We had a perfect spot for it. We had two nice bunks in the middle of the boat where a gentle draft of sweet-smelling air was coming through the cabin from the aft cockpit to keep us cool, then wafting out through the forward cockpit companionway. *Muskrat* needed no electric fans or air conditioning. Her natural ventilation was perfect.

Muskrat's tender. A handsome and efficient little "flattie" built before 1900, the skiff was just right for landing on a shallow beach. Photograph by the author. (Author's collection)

In due course Uncle Tod put down his book and took a peek out the opening port above his bunk. "All clear," he reported. So now we silently boarded the skiff and rowed a circuitous route over to Jones's citrus fruit stand a quarter mile back up the waterway. Indeed, we never bought more than two or three grapefruit at a time the entire cruise, because we never strayed far and the Jones's little dock was an ideal place to tie up the skiff and go ashore. And besides, Mrs. Jones was a lovely lady to chat with and discuss the conditions of the world and the local fruit business.

After exploring the trail that followed the shore, Uncle Tod observed that the sun was getting low and that it should be safe to return to *Muskrat*. So, keeping well clear of the *Puffin* and Mr. and Mrs. Clifford, we rowed out to our boat and climbed aboard, only to discover four beautiful sea trout lying on the cockpit seat.

What was to be done? Uncle Tod confidently suggested that when it got a bit darker we could just slip the fish over the side. Easy to say. But as we sat sipping our drinks of rum and key lime, I became aware that both of us kept making sidelong glances down at the silvery little angels. Finally, Uncle Tod broke off our conversation and said, "Hang it all, Waldo, I'll clean 'em if you'll cook 'em." With increasing enthusiasm we dined that evening on sea trout. And then we rowed over to *Puffin* to thank the Cliffords, and of course we stayed on for a spell and had a fine evening of talk about old times and old friends and our favorite boats.

The next morning, while lingering over our breakfast coffee, Uncle Tod asked me where I would like to go for the day. Almost without thinking I answered, "Aren't we there already?" "Yes," Uncle Tod said, "but I wasn't sure if you knew it." And so the following few delightful days flew by. And in the evenings, Uncle Tod and I often found ourselves in the little forward cockpit, a most convenient retreat for pleasant thoughts, quiet conversations, and a sense of detached peace. Way up in the eyes of our boat, sitting

Uncle Tod Swift's powerboat *Muskrat* at anchor in Snake Bird Cove, Florida, just north of Vero Beach on the east side of the Intracoastal Waterway. Photograph by the author. (Author's collection)

on comfortable seats, we had unrestricted views of starlit skies and still waters, enhanced here and there with a spot of light on shore or a boat passing in the distance. Surely *Muskrat* was a perfect boat for life in the southern portions of the Intracoastal Waterway.

Muskrat's general size and arrangement intrigued me so deeply that during the last couple of days aboard I went about the boat with a tape measure and a pad of paper jotting down general dimensions and specific details. On any thoughts for minor changes, I consulted Uncle Tod, and between us we modified little things here and there to achieve possible improvements. For instance, Uncle Tod suggested lengthening the main cockpit a tiny amount to make it a better fit for the skiff. I changed *Muskrat*'s transom berths to the Concordia type of folding berths. When I got back north I took my notes to naval architect and friend Fenwick Williams in Marblehead. With these measurements, Fenwick drew the sketch plan of *Muskrat II* as shown here. This dreamboat has not yet been built, but there's no time like the present.

In the fall of 1959 Uncle Tod called me to find out if he could leave *Tyche* with us at Concordia for the winter. At the time he was living at

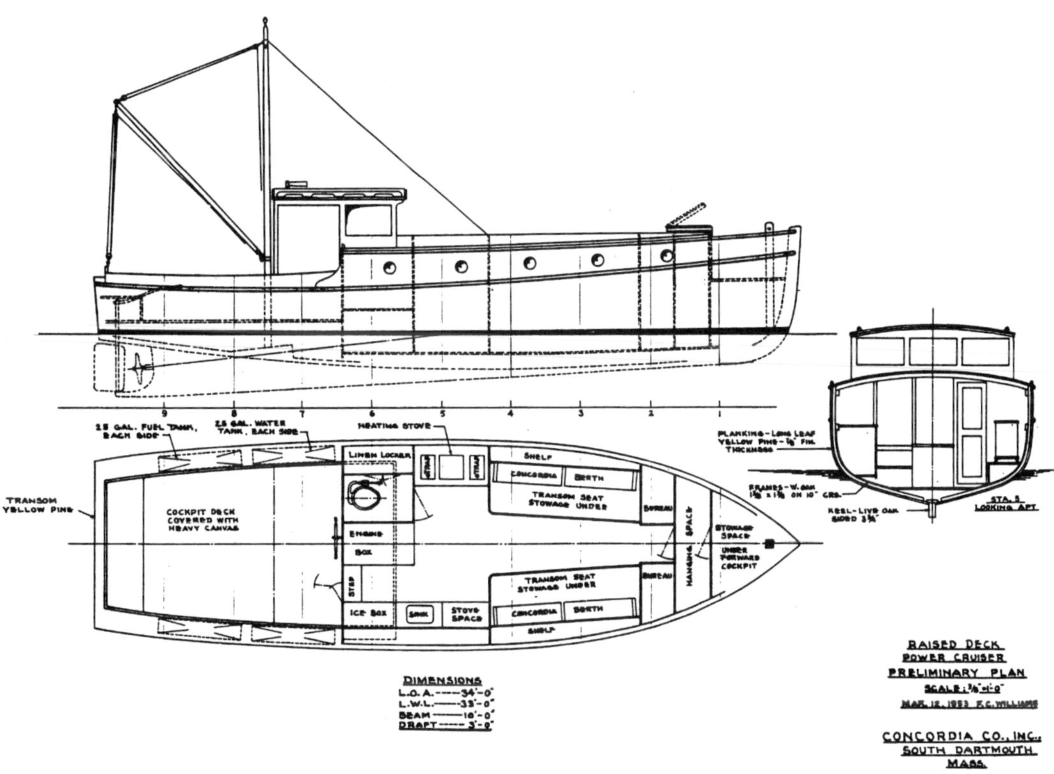

Using the author's measurements and Uncle Tod's recommended modifications, Fenwick Williams drew up this preliminary plan for *Muskrat II* in 1955. The 34' overall boat was designed to measure 33' on the waterline, with a 10' beam and 3' draft.

Chilmark in a frame cabin that he had built right next to his stone cabin in 1955. In season, *Tyche* was moored not far away in Quitsa Pond, a snug offshoot of the bigger Menemsha Pond.

Uncle Tod set a date and made arrangements for me to join him for the delivery trip across Vineyard Sound and Buzzards Bay. As usual everything was in good order, and we started our trip early in the morning. As we neared the busy little harbor of Menemsha Bight, I went below so that *Tyche* would be seen passing out through the jetties with her master alone, as usual, at the wheel.

At Concordia Uncle Tod gave us his instructions for the winter, said farewell to our crew, and left with his sister, Helen, for the ferry back to the Vineyard. That was the last I ever saw of him. Apparently he got back home safely, went to the post office to pick up his mail, had gotten into his car, and had started to light up his pipe, when a final stroke carried him off. A typically neat arrangement to the end.

Tyche stayed on with us at Concordia for many years. Agnes and Sally Swift were now her owners, and together we arranged that the Howlands would maintain the boat, the daughters would cruise in her whenever they could, and the Howland sons would sail her as she was available. What a

Tyche tied up in her summer port, the upper harbor of Menemsha Bight, with Menemsha Pond in the background, 1952. *Tyche* appears in several color postcards of Menemsha Bight that have been distributed throughout the United States. Photograph by Norman Fortier, neg. 5836. (Courtesy of the photographer)

wonderful setup it was! In due course *Tyche* taught all four of my boys about seagoing procedures and pleasures. We all have many memories of Uncle Tod and *Tyche* to pass on to the next generation.

Tyche was in due course ceremoniously broken up and buried on the same land upon which *Integrity* was built. As I have said before, good people and good pine trees do seem to live on in wondrous ways.

Enjoying the gentle breeze in Buzzards Bay, Kin Howland and a friend sail *Tyche* off the wind, with sheets started. The little schooner had 400 square feet of sail, with lazy jacks rigged for both main and foresail and ratlines on both main and foreshrouds. A fisherman's anchor swung under her bowsprit. In addition to good rails all around, lifelines could be run from the bow to the forestays and back to the mainstays and gallows frame. The big deckhouse forward was over the living quarters. The small house aft was over the engine room. *Tyche* had clear decks and a watertight cockpit. Framed in oak, planked in cypress, and decked with white pine, she was 27' overall (22' on the waterline), with a 9'6" beam and 4'6" draft. Photograph by Norman Fortier, neg. 12093. (Courtesy of the photographer)

3
Building *Integrity*

After I bought South Wharf in 1941 and got Concordia Company's boatyard up and running there, I fell into the habit of crossing the grounds of the New Bedford Yacht Club on my way to work. During the summer months there was always a group of sailors, amateur and professional, chatting by the club flagpole, waiting for the eight o'clock cannon that would announce the official start of another day of boating. These daily rituals were not only full of fun and laughter, but were also a fine source of yachting news and scuttlebutt.

Among the yacht captains who gathered by the yacht club flagpole in the years before World War II were Captain Harold Hardy, Herb Gelder, Olaf Rasmussen, John Christensen, Johnny Weeks, and that master of the tall tale, Captain Ben Waterworth. Another was my contemporary and particular friend, Tom Waddington.

Like my father and Uncle Tod Swift, Tom Waddington grew up on the New Bedford waterfront, by this time the home port for a big fishing fleet. His first boat was an abandoned skiff that he and his friends patched up and for which his mother made a sail out of the proverbial old sheet. According to gossip, their cruises in this noble craft were pretty venturesome, and Tom's boatbuilding skills surely developed at an early age. His next seafaring experience was a few years in the commercial fishery. By 1940, however, and for some years thereafter he worked as boatman for Seabury Stanton aboard the S.S. Crocker-designed New Bedford 35 sloop *Sea Breeze*. Tom also saw service in World War II, teaching navigation and ferrying army craft from here to there on the Intracoastal Waterway.

It is the winter of 1962-63, and *Integrity*'s framing is almost complete. Her fine bow sections and full sections above the waterline show to good advantage. We all studied the sheer line very carefully when the time came to make it final. The sheer shown on drawn plans can differ very materially from the sheer on the boat as built. Photograph by the author. (Author's collection)

Olad II, Tom Waddington's 47' schooner *Olad II* was built by H. Manley Crosby in 1928 as *Whistle Binkie*. At 35' on the waterline, she had a 12'6" beam, 5'9" depth of hold, and 6'6" draft. Tom used her for charter in both New England and Southern waters during the 1950s. She is shown on the ways at South Wharf, with Concordia foreman Martin Jackson painting from a yard skiff while Nick Demers and George Burns paint from the raft. Photograph by Norman Fortier. (Courtesy of the photographer)

Not long after the war he went into the yacht charter business, first buying an ancient English-built iron yawl, *Black Witch*, and later the Crosby-designed and -built schooner *Olad*. Trying to operate a charter business, with winter sailings in the Bahamas and Florida and summer sailings in New England waters, does not create a very good climate for continuing successful married life. Many boat-loving couples have tried it one way or another without success, and Tom was one of them.

But Tom ran a good ship in every way and was always busy. He was a rare combination of professional skill and amateur spirit. He was also a true jack of all trades. He wrote the annual Bahamas cruising guide. He became a sought-after deep-sea diver, and he was welcome at almost any shipyard as a temporary rigger, carpenter, or painter.

Tom was the best of shipmates to cruise or go to sea with, and for eight years running my wife, Katy, and I made annual trips with him down the Intracoastal Waterway to Palm Beach in the fall and back again in the spring to Southport, Connecticut. This was aboard Mrs. John Brooks's converted shrimp boat, *Uncle Jack*, which was some 65 feet long, had spacious living rooms on the upper deck and sleeping cabins below. Bikie Brooks was tourist guide and cook; Tom was captain, navigator, and mechanic; Katy and I were guests. But Katy was also dish and clothes washer, and I was part-time helmsman and dockline handler. It was all delightful and amounted to six weeks of cruising vacation each year. Tom is gone now. I surely miss him.

Uncle Tod Swift and Tom Waddington were godfathers of the schooner *Integrity*, but Robert D. Culler, best known as Pete, was unquestionably her primary architect. I first met Pete in 1940. My fiancée, Katy Kinnaird, and I were making an evening call on Charlie and Ing Mayo aboard their 43-foot Alden schooner *Blue Moon*, which was snugly tied up at the then-quaint little "city docks" in Fort Lauderdale, Florida. Pete and his wife, Toni, were aboard their yawl *Spray* a few yards upstream, and a hail from Charlie brought the Cullers over to join us. Down below in *Blue Moon*'s lamp-lit cabin we were soon absorbed in very basic and far-reaching nautical discussions, the essence of which have influenced my boat philosophy ever since.

Captain Tom Waddington (1910-92) at the wheel of Mrs. John Brooks's shrimper home, *Uncle Jack*. Unidentified photographer. (Author's collection)

Pete was about my age. Born in Oswego, New York, he had spent his school years in Santa Barbara, California. Like Charlie Mayo and me, he had always been engrossed in the world of boats and boating, and against all friendly advice to the contrary he was planning to make his living from boats. As early as 1929 he had with his own hands and for his own use built a substantial 36-foot yawl.

In planning this ambitious project he had made some very sound decisions. First, he chose the famous *Spray* for a model. Her owner, Joshua Slocum, was a uniquely able seaman and had proved the virtue of his yawl by successfully sailing her single-handed around the world. Next, for a building site, Pete chose the Eastern Shore of Maryland, because this was an area where small commercial vessels like *Spray* were still being built and used–and where there were still boatbuilders who knew how to build them. Furthermore, there was in the vicinity suitable lumber.

R.D. "Pete" Culler (1907-75) is shown here in his workshop, ca. 1965. Photograph by Norman Fortier, neg. 62301. (Courtesy of the photographer)

His choice of the shipyard at Oxford, Maryland, proved to be a splendid one. The owner, Alonzo R. Conley, was not only a well-known master builder but a worthy gentleman as well. He heartily approved of Pete's project and cooperated with Pete in its progress in every way, guiding and helping as asked or needed.

Conley also employed Pete during busy times at the yard and on special projects. This extra work helped Pete financially and at the same time instilled in him many of the skills and secrets useful for building traditional wooden boats soundly and economically. Needless to add, Pete's *Spray* as finished was a fine little ship and was soon in use as a home and as a year-round charter vessel. Like *Blue Moon*, *Spray* was available for charter in New England in the summer, in Florida and the Bahamas in the winter, and on the Chesapeake in the spring and fall. The two boats were, indeed, two of the better-known early charter boats in southern waters.

One of the yarns told that evening aboard *Blue Moon* concerned *Spray*'s annual trips up and down the Intracoastal Waterway. *Spray* apparently slipped along well under power. Compared to a big fancy powerboat, however, she was slow. To make a good day's run Pete would start early in the morning before breakfast and run until dark. The big fancy powerboat, on the other hand, found it more practical and less tiring to have breakfast at the marina, leave later in the morning, step right along and pass *Spray* about noon, and then arrive at the next logical spot in time to enjoy a happy hour before *Spray* hove into sight.

Rose Dolan's schooner *Defiance* measured 45' (37' on the waterline), with a 13'10" beam and 4'6" draft. She carried 1,160 square feet of sail. Designed by Murray Peterson and built by Paul Luke in 1960, *Defiance* did considerable cruising in Southern waters and in Europe, as well as in New England. Photograph by Norman Fortier, 1964, neg. 14810. (Courtesy of the photographer)

That's the way it went, which was fair enough by Pete. But occasionally, if it suited him and the weather was propitious, he would head *Spray* out one of the waterway cuts into the ocean and sail a direct course for 36 or more hours. This procedure would bring slow and easy *Spray* ahead of the speedy powerboat, much to the wonderment and dismay of the powerboat's owner. Of course, Pete's yarn is of no importance in itself, but it does indicate that Pete had a lovely sense of time and humor–and that *Spray*, handled with understanding, could comfortably, economically, and smartly, too, make a long passage. In any seafaring expedition, time is of vital importance in the long run, a fact Pete well understood.

Although I saw Pete occasionally after meeting him on *Blue Moon*, my next sustained contact with him came following the 1954 hurricane. We both happened to be in Menemsha Bight on Martha's Vineyard during Hurricane

Carol, he with a charter party aboard his newly acquired 52-foot Alden schooner *Rigadoon* and I with three of my sons on *Fetcher*, Concordia's 40-foot Nova Scotian lobster boat turned yard boat. *Fetcher* up in Quitsa Pond survived, but *Rigadoon* down in Menemsha Harbor became a total loss after Pete and his charter party made their way ashore. As there was no insurance on *Rigadoon*, Pete's charter business came to an abrupt end. As always, however, Pete soon found many projects to work on; some, fortuitously, for and with me.

In 1956, at my urgent appeal, he agreed to go aboard Miss Rose Dolan's new Concordia yawl, *Crisette*, as professional skipper and knowledgeable helper in her many boating plans. This turned out to be a very important decision for me, too, because it kept me in close contact with Pete for many years to come. He continued on with Miss Dolan through her ownership of *Crisette* and then of another similar-sized yawl, *Pellegrina*.

With *Pellegrina*, Miss Dolan wanted to try out one of the keel-centerboard boats that were then so popular in racing circles. Although she graciously gave Concordia the opportunity to design and build the boat for her, I was not really keen about this type and thought someone else could do better for her. Both Pete and I urged her to have the design work done by Aage Nielsen. Aage was a designer we thought very highly of, and for the next four years *Pellegrina* did very well in racing events.

Then Miss Dolan's focus changed quite suddenly. At Pete's suggestion she commissioned Murray Peterson to design for her a 45-foot shoal-draft coasting schooner in which she could do more live-aboard cruising. The *Defiance* was modeled after a series of very successful little clipper-bowed schooners designed by Peterson, among them *Coaster I* and *Coaster II*. I had the pleasant and useful experience of making the delivery trip aboard *Defiance* from Paul Luke's yard in East Boothbay, Maine, where she was built, to Padanaram in the late fall of 1960.

This couldn't have been a more timely pas-

Pete Culler's first sketch of my dreamship, *Integrity*. From the day Pete drew it, the sketch hung on Katie's and my bedroom wall, where we could study it and absorb its subtle lure. Obviously, the sketch shows the schooner just after the Howlands have rowed ashore to have a look around a small Caribbean island. However, we will be back on board shortly, because the headsails are only lowered, not furled, and the topsail, although not set, is still hanging at the topmast head. Captain Culler must be in charge, as only the long blue pennant is flying. An old coaster would not display yacht flags. (Author's collection)

sage, because earlier in 1960 Tom Waddington and I had been talking about an adventurous scheme in which I would build a schooner for charter and Tom would be the skipper and manager of the charter business. We would share income on some fair basis, and the Howland family would have some time aboard the schooner each year, probably during the winter months when the boatyard load would be least pressing. I guess I knew in my heart that the monetary profits from such an operation would be small or nonexistent. But the general idea was so tempting that I subconsciously rationalized in many directions.

Every plan has to begin somewhere. I started dreaming with Pete Culler about building a charter boat. Quick as a wink, out came his pencil. Before I knew it, there was our dream sketched out on paper. Katy and the children were all enthusiastic. So was I. But then, whammo, we ran into a serious stumbling block: Tom Waddington got married. We all agreed that it would be better and more prudent for Tom to become skipper on Miss Dolan's new schooner, *Defiance*, than to gamble on a charter experiment like mine.

In spite of losing Tom as skipper-manager I was so intrigued with the whole idea of building a little vessel that I kept on thinking and planning with Pete. As a first step we drove down to Maine in Pete's winter sand-weighted pickup truck to pay a call on Murray Peterson.

Murray treated us to a good lunch, then studied Pete's sketches and data, all of which he approved. He assured us that he would be delighted to design a coaster for us. But in the end he concluded that we were already on the right track, and he urged Pete to design the boat himself, especially as Pete was going to follow through with the building of her. So that was the way we left it: Pete Culler would design the schooner; Murray Peterson would help us whenever we wanted his assistance.

Where *Integrity* Was Built

Suitable space for building *Integrity* was not available at the Concordia boatyard in Padanaram. We therefore set the project up three miles to the south and west, next to the sheds where we built wooden Beetle Cats, on land that had once supported an ancestral Howland farm.

The big shed has a high main section for the storage of new Beetle Cats and for old ones that are awaiting repairs or other work. The north lean-to is for the actual building of new Beetles or the repair of others. The south lean-to is for painting them. From front to back (west to east), this three-part unit runs down a gentle slope from Smith Neck Road to a wooded area.

North of and parallel to the building and storage shed is the lumber storage with big doors facing south. Its post-and-beam construction means that the pine siding can be used vertically and thereby shed water without the need for tar paper or additional shingles. With this type of construction, air can breathe through the cracks between the boards, but rain stops on the edges of the boards and runs down and off at the bottom. Vertical boarding lasts many times longer than horizontal boarding. The lumber shed has been an excellent building for its job and is far enough from the building shed to leave an open, but protected area to work in.

This turned out to be a perfect location. The site was in the lee of a big shed that would protect our outside work from the cold north winter winds, and it was close by the big doors of the south leanto, in which there was ample space to set up machinery and mark out our mold loft floor. The leanto had many south windows for good light, and the doors were large enough to get bulky objects in and out with ease. Water and electricity were already in place.

The ground here sloped gently as it would do normally at a shoreside shipyard, and this made for good drainage in wet weather for both lumber storage and building operations. Importantly, the same slope made it possible to lay all blocking for the keel right on the ground. Higher blocking was not required to fit the keel contour. It was obviously helpful to keep the growing hull as close to the ground as possible, because this would permit lower staging to work from and less height for lifting heavy lumber and tools. Really, we could not have had a better setup.

Integrity's building site was just a few yards south (and to the right) of Concordia Company's Beetle Cat boat sheds on Smith Neck Road in South Dartmouth. Photograph by Norman Fortier. (Courtesy of the photographer)

Designing *Integrity*

Before Pete Culler could begin his formal design of the Howland schooner we had to establish some rough dimensions. As there were seven in our family, the ship needed to be large enough to accommodate eight people comfortably, preferably in three separate cabins. She also had to have a good full galley (with coal stove) and a separate compartment for engine and tanks. All this called for a length between perpendiculars of some 52 feet and, consonant with the general design and with pleasing proportions for passenger cabin and deck areas, a beam of 15 feet. I would have liked her to draw between five and six feet. However, to have included a centerboard would have added materially to the cost of both construction and future maintenance. So we settled on a fall keel and a draft of six feet, nine inches.

As to the rig, we had no special objectives except to follow the traditional fashion. It seemed reasonable to assume that, through the years, old-timers must have come to a good compromise between efficiency, ease of handling, and cost under a wide range of conditions. My only modification was a foresail that was slightly on the large size and a main slightly on the small size. I felt this change would make a very good rig for running before the wind, especially under shortened sail. Although a bigger mainsail would doubtless be more efficient for going to windward, it would in general be heavier to handle.

The next step was a builder's half model. This Pete Culler carved out and checked over with that highly experienced coasting seaman Captain Harold E. Hardy and others. In the model, Pete incorporated the fine lines and long run of a packet schooner. The long parallel deck lines and strong sheer are characteristic of most coasting schooners, whether designed for heavy cargo or light. Pete then took the lines of the model and transferred them first to paper and, in due course, scaled up to full size, on the mold loft floor.

Especially in these days of computers, I find it hard to explain the significance of half models in the designing of a boat. But in my limited understanding I still feel that they are of great value to a designer and to a prospective owner. In the old days a half model was almost essential before one started to build a full-scale boat. As to why a half model instead of a whole model, I can only suggest that since both sides of a boat should be the same, trying to carve out two identical sides would be both confusing and redundant. By using just one side, identical measurements can still be taken off for both sides.

Lines or measurements taken off the half model and drawn on paper produce plans for building purposes. These lines can be very accurate and can be read and well understood by naval architects and those with an experienced eye for them. But for many of us they can be confusing or at least not give us a complete picture. With a half model, on the other hand, a designer or owner can not only have a clear visual view from many angles, but can feel the shape of the boat-to-be by hand.

We can all, as an example, see a carving knife with our eyes. But to tell how sharp the knife is we usually (and very carefully) feel the edge with a finger. Similarly, to appreciate the texture of a piece of material we first look at it and then feel it with our hands. In other words, to feel as well as see a boat's shape can usually teach us some additional important factors that are not readily apparent to the eye alone. After all, a boat feels its way through the water, and the water tries to rub off any untoward bumps or shapes a hull possesses.

With Pete's half model lying on the table, I could pretty well understand what my shop would be like. Holding it in my hands I could feel it from all angles and pick up details that were not obvious to me as I looked at the lines on paper. With my eyes shut I could pretend that I was the famous blind John B. Hereshoff and get a reinforced understanding of my schooner-to-be. My fingers could feel the fine underwater bow sections, the long easy run of the aft underwater body, and the strong graceful sheer of the deck. There is no doubt that Pete Culler's half model helped to convince me that I was going to get the little ship I wanted.

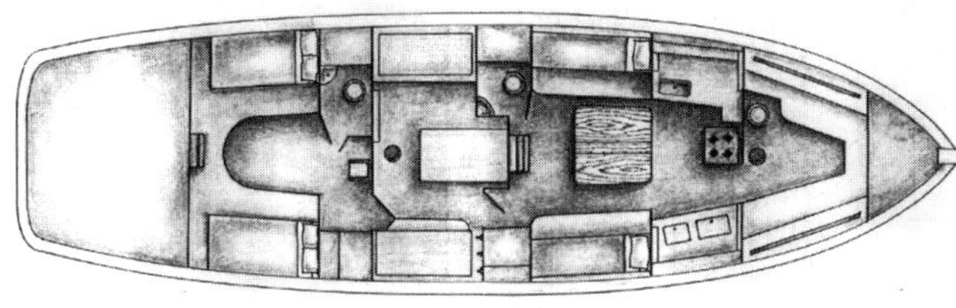

With the goal of sleeping eight persons in three separate cabins, including a good galley with coal stove and icebox, and placing the engine in a separate compartment, the final belowdecks arrangement came to this. The fo'c'sle contained berths for two; next aft came the full-width galley, followed by the main cabin where meals were served by day and at night four persons could sleep on a pair of upper and lower berths located out against the hull. (The practical, long-established custom of using the inboard portion of the lower berths as settees came in handy for daytime lounging as well as eating.) At the aft end of the main cabin were a hanging locker to starboard and an enclosed head (toilet room) to port. Between these spaces sat the diesel engine, boxed in, but projecting into a generous, full-width engine room with fuel tanks outboard. Aft of the engine, as the last of the living spaces, was the aft cabin with berths for two, its own enclosed head, hanging lockers, and a small heating stove for chilly weather. In an arrangement similar to the main cabin, settees were provided inboard of the berths in traditional horseshoe fashion. The owner (or charterer) who normally occupied this cabin could, through a companionway in the aft end of the deckhouse, enjoy direct and independent access to the deck above. Drawn by Kathy Bray.

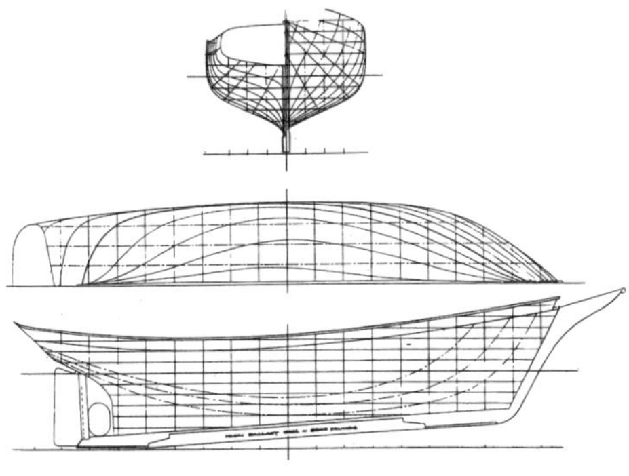

These lines represent, in the two dimensions of a page, the shape of our schooner's hull. Although it has long been common practice for designers to create such a drawing from a blank sheet of drawing paper and so establish a hull shape, Pete Culler, who designed our schooner, started with only a rough sketch and from it carved a half model that represented, in small scale, what he had in mind. After designer and owner had studied the model from many angles and approved its shape, Pete then took its measurements and from them created this drawing. By use of such a model, a better understanding of the shape of the completed vessel can be obtained—at least for those not able to visualize directly from drawings.

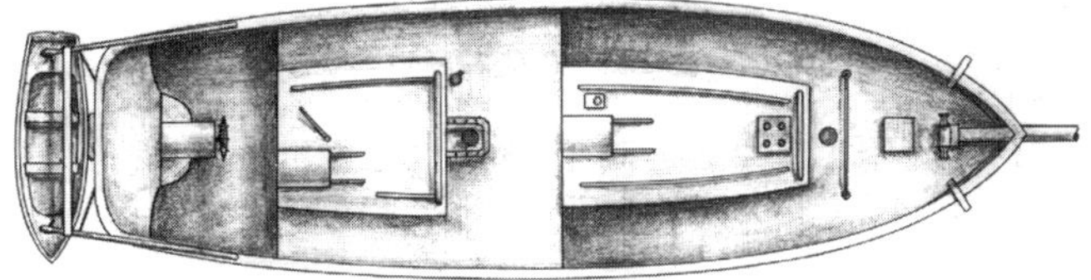

The schooner's design called for a two-level deck, with the main deck and aft deck sunken below the rails where the surrounding bulwarks gave security and a feeling of being in the vessel instead of on it. A raised quarterdeck over the aft cabin and engine room provided more useful headroom beneath. Two deckhouses, one rising from the foredeck between the masts and the other built atop the quarterdeck, allowed full standing headroom under them in the desired areas. Hatches through the deck located way forward and way aft gave access to the chain locker in the forepeak and the ship stores in the lazarette aft, respectively. There was also a hatch over the galley cookstove so the heat could escape in warm weather. In time-honored schooner fashion, catheads projected from the port and starboard bows for hoisting the anchors aboard, while a pair of davits ran beyond the stern for lifting out the yawlboat. Other deck-related items consisted of an anchor windlass mounted on the pawlpost at the aft end of the bowsprit, a staysail traveler, an abundance of handrails attached to the top edges of the deckhouses, and, of course, the wheelbox aft at the head of the rudderstock. Drawn by Kathy Bray.

Tools

Special tools for building a sawn-frame vessel are not numerous, but some of them must be quite massive compared to those found in a small yacht yard. We spent some time looking for the big three essentials. First was a secondhand makeshift ship's bandsaw we found at the Peirce and Kilburn shipyard in nearby Fairhaven. It was not perfect—in fact, we called it the Bitch Kitty—but it served our purposes. We also found a big thickness planer—secondhand, from a box factory—and a jointer we bought through a machinery broker. We ourselves made up the roller stands needed to help guide and carry the heavy frame stock across the saw table.

A ship's saw has a canting or tilting head that allows the timbers being shaped to roll forward on a level saw table, while the saw itself changes angles as the timbers pass through to achieve the desired beveled shapes. The jointer we used to flatten one face of a rough-sawn timber before putting it through the thickness planer. We also used it to straighten the edges of boards or planks. A thickness planer dresses rough-sawn timber such as hull planking or decking to a desired uniform thickness. The planer had to be rugged enough to bring big rough stock down to uniform thickness with a minimum number of passes under the rotating knives. Although they are powered nowadays by individual electric motors, these machines were originally powered through line shafting and flat leather belts driven by a large single electric motor.

Other old-fashioned tools we used in building *Integrity* included a heavy vise (it came off a whaleship) and a dozen big ship's C-clamps that Dana Story of Essex, Massachusetts, very generously let us have. It gave us a rewarding feeling of historical continuity to think that our clamps had been used in building many of the famous Gloucester fishing schooners. The clamps are now in use at the Mystic Seaport Shipyard.

We used three electric tools that the oldtimers did not have. First was a portable Skil saw that would cut lumber three inches thick. As all *Integrity*'s frame stock was three inches, this saved a great deal of hand sawing and heavy lugging. Second was a portable Skil plane with a rotating cutter that eliminated consuming hand planing of heavy timbers. Third was a set of electric drills to bore for the fastenings and bungs.

As for other basic tools we used, the adzes, hand planes, mauls, and chisels were all much the same as had been used in the old days. These belonged for the most part to the individual workers, all of whom took great pride in owning them. As my friend Major William Smyth used to tell me, you can learn a lot about a carpenter's abilities by looking at his tool box.

Lumber

With one or two exceptions the lumber that we used grew locally, by which I mean within 20 or so miles of South Dartmouth. The frame stock was all white or yellow-bark oak. It came for the most part from a wooded valley in nearby Tiverton, Rhode Island. Here, protected by surrounding hills and the good management of a local gun club, the trees had not been damaged by hurricanes or casual cutting.

Gray's Sawmill was close at hand and was of absolutely vital importance to the success of the schooner project. Mr. Gray himself knew and understood boatbuilding woods. He started work on our lumber list right after the first fall frosts so that the sap would be down and out of the wood. He carefully selected the trees for our job, then milled them to the best advantage. In this way we acquired the natural crooks and sweeps for our frames, deck beams, and knees, as well as long straight-grain stock for the keel timber and the bilge and sheer clamps, etc. He landed the oak at our building site in early winter, and we started work on it as soon as practical, so that the wood could season in its finished form and with the help of winter snows and rains furnished by Mother Nature. It was my assignment to further the process, and help keep the wood from developing checks while drying, with continuing coats of linseed oil thinned (to promote penetration) with kerosene. My official title soon became Oiler Howland.

During lumber-collection months I spent as much time as I could spare at Gray's Sawmill, because I was fascinated by the sawing operation. To me this was like Christmas every day. As the big four-foot-diameter circular saw sliced through a noble oak log, it clearly revealed the tree's history, its structure, its grain and color, and of course its own special shape. As a matter of fact, it was while I watched this beautiful wood being sawn that the name *Integrity* first came into my mind. Natural material like this is *integrity* itself.

I often wondered what the forest god had grown a particular tree for. Would he be pleased that it was going to live on as part of a little ship? Or would he be sad to see it cut down in the prime of its life?

Although white pine for decks and cabin joinerwork came from a different area, it too was cut in the early winter and stuck (that is, piled in layers with stickers placed transversely between each layer) outside to air dry until needed the following summer. Mature trees were selected as having more heartwood and less sapwood than younger growth. The ship's lower bottom planks were oak, but for upper planking and cabin houses we used hard pine, no doubt originating from Georgia, that had already served well for many decades as framing in the Sylvia Ann Howland School in New Bedford. For the rudder we imported a big timber of greenheart. Rudders are subjected to considerable strain and often become worn, allowing seaworms to get in. Greenheart grows in tropical areas and is heavy, strong, and largely impervious, I am told, to worms.

Fastenings

For fastenings and most of *Integrity*'s hardware, we used only galvanized iron. The one exception was rudder hardware: gudgeons and pintles were of cast bronze.

Although the old vessels did not usually have outside ballast keels, I asked Pete Culler to figure on one for *Integrity*. My thinking was that it would eliminate some bulky inside ballast and also serve as a good buffer against coral heads or granite rocks, should we accidently strike any. *Integrity*'s cast iron ballast keel was some 25 feet long, and the exposed deadwood that extended forward and aft of it was protected with one-inch galvanized plating. The keel bolts were 1-1/2-inch diameter; by the time they extended through the iron keel, the wood keel, the blocking between frames, and the keelson, they got to be some three feet long. This all made for an extremely strong backbone, which is a big factor in the long life of a vessel. The old workboats, even the small ones, usually had very heavy structural keel assemblies.

We made our own drifts and many of the other bolts from a good stock of galvanized iron rod and clinch rings. A big heavy boltcutter and the ship's vise were in constant use. In this way we lost no time waiting for bolts of the right length and diameter to come in from outside suppliers. The plank fastenings we chose were old-fashioned chisel-pointed square galvanized nails with a heavy head. Once they have been driven into sound oak and have set for awhile, these nails are almost impossible to draw out. Today's, iron fastenings are often brittle and of inferior quality. However, the ones we used appeared to be relatively soft and not easily broken. The galvanizing was excellent.

Launching

Integrity's launching day is still vivid in my memory. Not all work below decks or aloft had been completed, but the topsides and bottom had been properly painted to see her through the winter. It was already mid-December, and I had watched Mr. Loranger and his two great ten-ton cranes load our vessel on his long lowbed, then drag her over a short temporary gravel road to the paved road of Round Hill and finally down to the coffer-

Building *Integrity*

Squaring away for the construction of *Integrity*, with the south lean-to of Concordia's Beetle Cat building shed in the background. *Integrity*'s construction crew averaged five men, under the supervision of Pete Culler. The regular crew, young and old, stayed on for the duration of the project. From time to time we borrowed additional workers from Concordia Company or elsewhere. It was a challenging and interesting job for everyone involved. (Photographs in this sequence are by the author.)

View of building site from uphill on the west side. *Integrity*'s stem, keel, and sternpost are being assembled into her backbone. The snow is all to the good, helping the oak timbers to season in their final shape.

Arranging and checking the blocking before *Integrity*'s backbone is set in its perpendicular position. This insures that waterlines will be level and the keel line will be parallel to the slope of the ground. By keeping the vessel as low to the ground as possible during construction, the crew minimizes the need for tall ladders or staging—or for lifting heavy materials to excessive heights. The soil foundation is more forgiving than cement and thus easier on fallen tools—or workers, for that matter.

Integrity's stem, stem knee, wood keel, deadwood, and sternport are now set up and firmly stayed to hold the units in their proper perpendicular and level position. With stands of trees aft and to the east and south, a hill to the west, and the big Beetle Cat shed to the north, the building site is well sheltered. With ample space available for them inside the lean-to, the crew keep fully employed in fair weather or foul.

Integrity's middle frame assembly is the first one to be set on the keel. Here it is shown being plumbed up with great care. A gin pole hoists the heavy frame into final position. The tank in the foreground holds kerosene to be mixed with linseed oil and applied to each frame as it is set, and at weekly intervals thereafter. This was my responsibility. I did the work whenever possible on clear days with the wind in the northwest.

View of the vessel from just aft of the sternpost and propeller aperture. As frames continue to be set up from amidships towards both bow and stern, temporary battens are attached to keep all frames square to the center line, parallel to each other, and perpendicular. Shores from the ground are added to hold the frames in place during construction, and plumb bobs hang from stem and sternpost to indicate any deviation. The cross members between the frame tops are not the final deck beams. They are merely temporary cross-spalls to hold the frames in shape during the early phases of construction.

The schooner's frames are now nearing the sternpost. The horn timbers have been beveled off to a point to accommodate the transom, and the aft end of the ballast keel is visible. The final trimming of the frame tops will not take place until the sheer clamps and clamp shelves are in place.

View looking forward, showing *Integrity*'s deep and narrow forefoot below the water. Frames continue across the keel here and make for great strength in a critical area. The forward upper end of the deadwood shows in the foreground.

The double frames as they cross over the deep keel. Many shores secure the hull's shape until fore-and-aft members and deck beams can be put in place.

Once started, the framing of *Integrity* went rapidly. Here the completed frame rests level on the sloping ground, as the completed vessel would rest in the water. The square box-like structure is the tank for tanbarking sails. The gin pole will remain standing at the site until all heavy timbers and fittings are in place.

View of *Integrity* completely framed, from the leanto roof.

Planking begins with the wale strake or sheer plank at the deck level and the garboard plank at the keel, then continues toward the middle or shutter plank, which will be the last plank to be fitted.

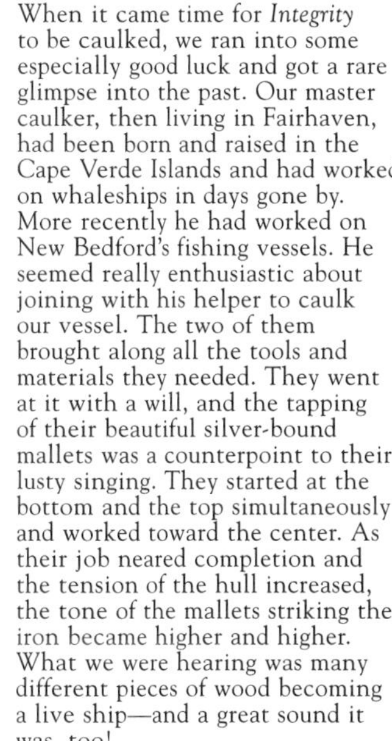

When it came time for *Integrity* to be caulked, we ran into some especially good luck and got a rare glimpse into the past. Our master caulker, then living in Fairhaven, had been born and raised in the Cape Verde Islands and had worked on whaleships in days gone by. More recently he had worked on New Bedford's fishing vessels. He seemed really enthusiastic about joining with his helper to caulk our vessel. The two of them brought along all the tools and materials they needed. They went at it with a will, and the tapping of their beautiful silver-bound mallets was a counterpoint to their lusty singing. They started at the bottom and the top simultaneously and worked toward the center. As their job neared completion and the tension of the hull increased, the tone of the mallets striking the iron became higher and higher. What we were hearing was many different pieces of wood becoming a live ship—and a great sound it was, too!

I spoke to the old gentleman one morning when he was caulking the deck up forward. He told me that he was doing an especially good job up there because he planned to ship on *Integrity* for a trip back home. In due course, *Integrity* did visit the Cape Verdes, but I guess the old caulker couldn't wait for our departure.

Three heavy wale strakes and a guard rail extend downward from the frame ends. These thick planks add great strength to the hull where it is in the greatest danger of crushing pressure when lying a wharf or coming into contact with another vessel.

The planks all have to be shaped in pairs, one for the starboard side, a mirror-image one for the port side. The garboard planks next to the keel are especially wide at the forward and after end of the hull. Other planks have less shape, but all must be planned carefully to take the proper curve on the hull and maintain a visually "right" sweep from bow to stern.

Planking is an art. Whoever lays out a plank must know his business if the job is to go well and quickly. There are tricks to be learned from every shape of hull, and Pete Culler, who was an expert at laying out planking, as well as framing, knew them all. As planking progresses, planks must be drilled to receive fastenings, and bungs must be made and driven in to plug the fastenings. Shoring and staging change constantly as the process moves along.

The inside of the hull is sheathed or ceiled with planking too. Unlike planking, sheathing is made of boards of uniform width. In addition to adding considerable stiffness and strength to the structure of the vessel, the sheathing creates an air space between itself and the planking that insulates for sound, heat, and cold. It also promotes ventilation and contributes to healthy conditions for man, cargo, and vessel throughout the hull.

The sheathing is nearly completed. Looking aft.

Integrity's deck beams, looking forward, while I look aft from the knightheads, the strengthening timbers at the bow that reinforce the structure and are pierced for the anchor chain hawseholes. The sturdy mast partners, where the foremast will pass through the deck, is visible amidships.

With the planking completed, frame heads await cutting to finished length. Inside, the schooner's clamp and shelf are in place to add further stiffening and to support the ends of the deck beams, which have been installed. The voids amidships and aft are where the two cabins will be located. Her bottom has been tarred, and her topsides have received a primer coat of light gray oil-based paint. I am sitting in the knightheads right forward.

Installation of quarter-deck beams, looking aft.

With the quarter-deck beams in place, planking is about to commence. The wide waterways that define the outside margins of the planking have been installed. The aft deck house is in place, but not finished. I am not as apprehensive as I appear here.

Deck, waterways, and rails completed, as well as both houses. The turned stanchions for the monkey rail around the stern deck are perpendicular to the hull and thus cant forward slightly. They also cant inboard following the tumblehome of the hull. This is not only correct in shipbuilding terms, but it keeps the rail clear of contact with docks and with vessels rafting alongside *Integrity*. It also looks right. First hull contact with a piling will be by the guard rail at deck level on the hull.

The main cabin house is now completed, as is taffrail, and diaphragm pump has been installed, as have the main pinrail and the traveler for the foresail sheet block to slide. Two deadlights set into the quarterdeck give light to the engine room. The forward-facing lights on the aft cabin trunk have slides to protect them in heavy weather.

Integrity's steering wheel was built by Concordia's master carpenter and cabinet maker Leslie Randall, a noted specialist in the art of wooden steering wheel-making.

dam dock. Here, the same place from which the whaleship *Charles W. Morgan* had been refloated some 20 years before, *Integrity* had been waiting for a high tide and a smooth sea. The tides had come and gone with their meticulous regularity, but continuing heavy winds had worn our patience to the breaking point. Real winter would soon be upon us. We had to get our ship over to Concordia's protected basin–and soon!

At last a favorable chance showed up, as it usually does once a week during the cold months and after a strong northwesterly wind shows signs of weakening. Mr. Loranger arrived late in the afternoon and set up his cranes to try a launching early the next morning. *Integrity* was already positioned parallel to the dock and as close to the west side of it as possible. The lift would thereby be nearly straight up over some wharf pilings. Lowering into the water would be more worrisome, because the crane booms would then have to reach further and, possibly, create a tip-over situation. After the 1954 hurricane I had watched a crane drop Henry Morgan's 62-foot cutter *Djinn* in mid-launching off the Padanaram bridge. The load was too heavy, and the crane operator had to release his load to save his equipment and himself from going overboard with *Djinn*. Pete Culler worried, too, but about his weight calculations. Would *Integrity* float where she was supposed to?

Nervous minutes passed like hours. But when the moment came, the launch went perfectly. All of a sudden our vessel was alive, floating like a duck just as she should. Soon Pete and I were aboard *Integrity*, and Martin Jackson on our towboat *Fetcher* passed us a line. We were on our way to Padanaram. It was one of those marvelous times in life when everything seems to be looking up. The morning was crisp and beautiful. The sun was rising before us even as the moon set astern. The sea was calm, save for a long, gentle surge that gave our ship a lovely motion of weightless progress.

Securely loaded onto a flatbed truck, *Integrity* is ready to travel to her launching. Photograph by Norman Fortier, neg. 14112. (Courtesy of the photographer)

Once we had *Integrity* tied up under the derrick in Concordia's basin our crew commenced a winter of finishing up jobs, stepping the masts, making up and installing the rigging, completing the interior, and outfitting it with plumbing, stove, cabin heater, and the like. At the same time the engine was installed and all the wiring and controls were put into place.

Spars

As was customary, *Integrity*'s three main spars–mainmast, foremast, and bowsprit–were solid eastern white pine. Back in 1941, my friend

William G. Saltonstall published *Ports of the Piscataqua*, a most interesting book about coastal New Hampshire in colonial days and the procuring of white pine for the Royal Navy. It seems that these eastern white pines made very good masts for sailing ships, being not too heavy and very durable. They often outlasted two ships. My thinking was that if white pine was good

In an exciting moment for designer, owner, and builders, *Integrity* is about to be launched into the coffer dam at Round Hill from which the whaleship *Charles W. Morgan* had been freed some 21 years earlier. In order to lift the boat over the pilings, the crane booms had to be canted further over the water than they are shown here. Photograph by the author.

After *Integrity* was secured under the derrick in the Concordia basin, the yard crew began a winter of finishing up carpentry jobs, stepping the masts, making up and installing the rigging, completing the interior, and outfitting the vessel with plumbing, stove, cabin heater, and all the other necessary gear. At the same time, the engine was installed by Jimmy Archer and all the wiring and controls were completed. Photograph by Norman Fortier, neg. 13693. (Courtesy of the photographer)

enough for nations to go to war over, it might be good enough for my schooner.

We actually cut three beautiful white pines on town water department land in South Dartmouth: one for the foremast, one for the main, and one for the bowsprit. With adze and plane our crew shaped them to eight sides and then to round. With the help of linseed oil and kerosene and daily sunlight, these spars seasoned themselves right in the boat. Then we slushed them down twice in the traditional way with petroleum grease.

For all other spars we used small, straight spruce trees grown in New Hampshire. These we painted using white lead and oil.

Rigging

Integrity's standing rigging was heavy galvanized iron wire, parceled with cotton cloth, oiled, and then served with houseline (which is similar to marlin but three-strand and heavier). The whole was then covered with Stockholm tar. With a few exceptions, the lower ends of each stay was turned back on itself around a deadeye and thimble and seized with stainless-

Integrity under power during her first sea trials off Padanaram, spring 1963. Photographs by Norman Fortier, neg. 13809. (Courtesy of the photographer)

At the crosstrees. Photograph by Kinnaird Howland. (Courtesy of the photographer)

steel wire. Only a portion of the head gear and topmast rigging was spliced. The headstay was double, with a throat seizing aloft, and the ends came down through cheeks on the bowsprit end and turned through a heart plate that was shackled to the chain bobstay. The servings on the shrouds not only protected them but simplified the installation of ratlines.

The spectacle eyes for fastening jib and staysail luffs to the stays were the old-fashioned type–and indeed were stock leftover from whaleship days. They had no tendency to stick or catch going up or coming down, and they were big enough to include the downhaul line. I had been told that deadeyes and lanyards in place of turnbuckles would be troublesome, but I wanted to adhere to the old methods and so went to the trouble of getting from England the right four-strand Italian hemp for the lanyards. I can say that we set the lanyards up in April for the first time, then again in June, and that was all for the first season. Not only were the lanyards tarred, but they were further protected and lubricated with beef tallow.

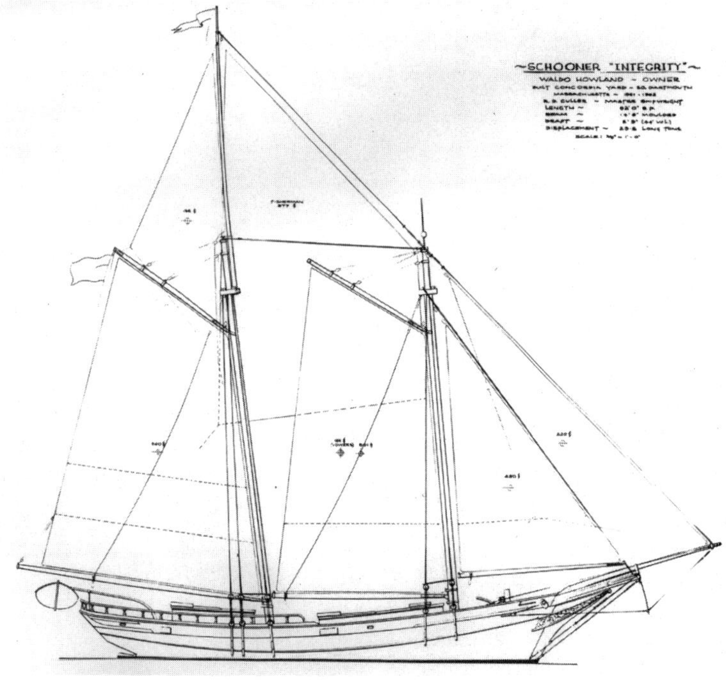

Integrity's sail plan. *Integrity*'s extra-large foresail, we figured, would help pull her downwind, making steering easier on such a point of sail, and in long passages we would be able to set a reefed mainsail, which, in effect, converted the rig to a ketch, and would ease steering even more. By contrast, when running downwind, schooners carrying big their mainsails way aft as shown in the lower drawing, tend to round up and are more difficult to keep on course. Drawing by R.D. Culler. (Author's collection)

All halyards and sheets on *Integrity* were manila, which has the disadvantage of shrinking with dampness. However, as *Integrity*'s booms and gaffs were free to slide on their jaws up and down the mast, the halyards could be left set up without fear of damage from shrinking.

The tiller ropes were linen soaked in hot tallow. Once set up they worked freely without any sign of wear or slacking for a full season.

Engine

The selection of a power plant for the schooner was a difficult one for me, since internal combustion had never been a great interest of mine and my knowledge of engines is very limited. A number of engines offered efficiency, reliability, and good dealer service. But in addition I hoped to get an

Installation of *Integrity*'s 100 h.p. Westerbeke diesel. Concordia's great mechanic Jimmy Archer guides the engine over the engine room hatchway. Photograph by Norman Fortier, neg. 13693. (Courtesy of the photographer)

engine that had a pleasing sound and disposition, rather than one that gave a hurried buzz of impatience. What I had in mind was an old-fashioned, heavy-duty, slow-turning crude-oil engine. Fortunately, though, I was talked and reasoned out of this position. The modern six-cylinder 100-hp Westerbeke diesel that was ultimately installed in *Integrity* turned out to be most satisfactory. With a 3:1 reduction, it turned a 28-inch, three-blade propeller and drove *Integrity* at a cruising speed of seven knots.

Seven feet of fore-and-aft length is a lot for a small pleasure boat to reserve for an engine room, but it did make the job of maintenance easy and solved the problem of where to locate tanks, fire protection systems, tools, generators, and batteries. And with tanks in the middle of the boat there was never a problem of trim, whether the tanks were full or empty.

What a Coasting Schooner Offers

Perhaps the biggest challenge in planning a new boat is to know and keep clearly in mind what qualities and characteristics you most want. The temptation is to fool yourself into believing that with ingenuity and money you can have everything. There are many desirable features that a coasting schooner obviously lacks. Trying to graft these features onto *Integrity*'s design and layout would have compromised the good characteristics that have evolved through the many decades that these vessels were in active use.

Primarily, I wanted a boat that we as a family could live comfortably aboard for a number of weeks at a time. *Integrity* was such a boat. The plans show good living space below, not only for the necessary number of berths, but also for a workable galley, a combined tank, engine, and work room, and one comfortable double cabin separated from the other living quarters. There is space for the stowage of coal, supplies, and provisions, and space just to move in comfortably.

There was no need for extra insulation in the vessel; her construction is insulation in itself. And the heavy planking and pine sheathing with the air space in between provide insulation from sound as well as from heat and cold; just as the thick pine decks do. The strong sheer of the deck line and the location and shape of the deck houses and openings lend themselves to good natural ventilation. There is little or no trouble from condensation or dampness. Linens, foods, and other gear can be left aboard for extended periods whether the boat is lived in or not.

On deck, too, the coasting schooner offers comfortable and practical day-to-day living. The decks are wide and uncluttered and at a reasonable height above water for getting aboard from a dinghy or from the water after a swim. The high rails make a natural barrier to prevent things from blowing or falling overboard. The houses make natural seats everywhere. The raised deck stops water from coming aft. The steerage is an ideal back porch, complete with high stanchion rails aft and on each side. The aft cabin serves as a table for navigation gear and charts–and for the afternoon tea tray. It also makes a fine windbreaker.

Underway, with Tom Howland at the helm, the main boom and gaff have been hauled up enough to provide a clear view forward. The boom is vanged over to port to further assist the helmsman's vision. The horizontal gearshift lever can be seen on the aft cabin top. Photograph by Kinnaird Howland. (Courtesy of the photographer)

Integrity's booms and rigging are ideally located for awnings or clotheslines. The shape of the vessel tends to deflect strong winds from deck areas; it also results in a vessel that lies quietly at anchor with little bobbing up and down or swinging from side to side. The nearly parallel sides and heavy guard rails are as suitable today for lying to a dock as they were in the old days when cargo had to be loaded aboard.

The broad transom with suitable davits provides the best solution for carrying and using a yawlboat. A good dinghy that rows and sails well is, after all, one of the most essential pieces of equipment for any cruising boat, but if the boat is difficult to launch or stow, much of its utility is lost.

A second basic quality I wanted was a good seaboat that could sail to distant places safely and economically and be a pleasure to be aboard in the process. *Integrity* could do this well when she was handled with understanding. She had a slow, easy motion. As the swordfisherman said, "She will never dive, not with those apple cheek bows." Although not especially

View of the rigging, looking forward from the cockpit along the starboard waterway. Note that the deck is clear except for the jib sheet running aft from the knightheads through the fairleads. This was the only one of the four lower sheets that needed tending while tacking to windward. A topmast backstay, with tackle showing, hangs from the main shroud. Photograph by Kinnaird Howland. (Courtesy of the photographer)

beamy for her length, she did have great bearing forward and aft, and this tended to keep her sailing upright, not at a large angle of heel. This easy, level motion made living aboard more pleasant and less tiring for all hands, including the cook.

Steering was not a problem on *Integrity*. She would steer herself hour after hour on almost any point of sailing. This was an essential quality in the days when coasting schooners operated shorthanded. Even when running free in a strong breeze and following sea, *Integrity* would take care of herself under foresail and a close-trimmed jib. Under ordinary storm conditions she would heave-to comfortably under foresail, reefed or not, and backed staysail.

I am often asked if *Integrity* would go to windward. My answer is, "Yes, but she sure hated to." Especially in a big, short sea. There were times when this could be exasperating, but long trips to windward are discouraging under the best of circumstances in any kind of sailing vessel and can generally be avoided. The small area of *Integrity*'s sail plan (even the mainsail had less than 600 square feet) greatly eased the challenge of sailing her in a heavy breeze, her sails and were easy to hoist again after reefing. With the non-slippery soft linen sails and lazyjacks, and the sail gaskets always hung from the booms, we had little trouble shortening sail or furling.

It is difficult truthfully to claim that any pleasure boat today can be economical, but *Integrity* did keep cruising costs within some bounds. The very fact that she could sail meant a saving in fuel. She could be grounded out if necessary, rather than having to be hauled on a railway. Her deck gear and rigging were all of a kind that a seagoing crew could cope with and even take pleasure from. There was enough room in the paint locker for a coil or two of manila, and this took care of most of the likely replacements to running rigging that might be needed. With the exception of the main engine, there was very little mechanical gear that required specialized attention. As a coasting schooner, *Integrity* got along just fine with simple equipment.

A final thought, vague in form, had been in my mind while we planned and built *Integrity*. I knew that if I built a fast powerboat, I could expect to meet other owners of fast powerboats and to come in contact with different engine manufacturers and suppliers specializing in fast powerboats. Or, if I built a 12-Meter sloop I would meet other owners interested in international racing. So I reasoned that I, with a true coasting schooner, might meet a few of the oldtimers who had similar projects in mind, and other individualists who were interested in wooden ships and traditional ways. *Integrity* did not let me down in this hope, either, as should become clear from the following account of her first eight years of life.

Sails

I wanted linen sails for *Integrity*, but linen was obtainable only in Scotland. I also wanted the sails tanbarked, a process that was no longer available in this country, except in a small way by Concordia Company. The Scottish firm of Gowen & Company still made linen sails and had them tanbarked for fishing boats, so Gowen appeared to be the logical place to turn to. Through the cooperation of our friends at Manchester Yacht Sails in South Dartmouth, we sent Gowen *Integrity*'s sail plans and specifications, and I was delighted with the results.

The sails fitted well without alteration. They were easy on the eyes. They absorbed little water. They were soft to handle and easy to furl. Crosscut Dacron sails would have been more efficient under some conditions, but then a 12-Meter sloop would have been better for racing around the buoys.

Integrity's schooner rig gave her a variety of sail combinations to suit weather conditions. Her full rig for light air included a triangular main topsail above the main gaff and a quadrilateral fisherman staysail on the main topmast stay above the foresail. Her working rig of "four lowers" included jib, forestaysail, foresail, and mainsail. With mainsail reefed and jib furled she had the equivalent of a ketch rig, easily handled by a small crew. When it breezed up further we could double-reef the main and single-reef the foresail for a smaller ketch configuration. If it really came on to blow, *Integrity* could be hove to with reefed foresail and staysail. With staysail sheeted to weather she would nearly sail herself, the foresail pushing her up into the wind, the staysail making her fall off again. With four lowers only, *Integrity* was under-rigged, but could be driven hard reaching and running. With topsail, which handled easily from the deck, and the fisherman staysail, she would slip along in good shape.

Integrity under sail with four lowers and main gaff topsail, but without the fisherman staysail. Photograph by Norman Fortier, neg. 14101. (Courtesy of the photographer)

Integrity sailing from Padanaram in 1963 with a family group on board. This is one of the best and prettiest photographs ever taken of the schooner. Photograph by Norman Fortier, neg. 14100. (Courtesy of the photographer)

4
Chartering *Integrity*

The spring of 1963 was no different for me than any other boatyard spring. It was the same old anxious race to get boats ready for owners who had been planning all through cold winter evenings to get out on the water again in June–or earlier. May in New England, as my father used to say, "is forever the month of broken promises." It is bad enough to be late on any business contract. To delay a friend's weekend cruise is inexcusable. And so I had little time to worry about *Integrity* and preparations for her first season of chartering. Nevertheless, *Integrity* became for the Howlands a lucky ship.

I had envisioned short charters in local waters for the first summer, in order to get acquainted with the new schooner and to iron out any problems with her or her crew. It didn't work out that way. Our first stroke of good fortune was Captain Hardy's desire to make one more trip down to his home in Deer Isle, Maine, as skipper of a coasting schooner. Captain Hardy knew my sons Kin and Tom well and was happy to sign them on as mate and cook respectively. His first advice to them when they came aboard was typical and to the point. "Now, boys," he said, "you do just what I tell you, and we'll get along just fine." And that is the way it worked out. On a ship one captain is enough.

An equally fine charter schedule developed, almost by itself. Colonel Arthur Herrington, a longtime Concordia yawl owner and friend, asked to charter *Integrity* for the first part of the summer. His plan was to sail over to Newport to take in the start of the 1963 Transatlantic Race, then take a leisurely slide Down East for the annual Cruising Club of America cruise that was to start in Maine in mid-July. The charter was all in the family, so to speak. Captain Hardy had gone with Colonel Herrington aboard his new Concordia *Auda* as professional skipper

Captain Harold E. Hardy at the wheel of *Integrity*. A native of Deer Island, Maine, who as a boy and young man had sailed in coasting schooners, Captain Hardy served as professional skipper on my father's Concordia yawl *Java* for 17 years. He was captain on *Integrity* for her first sailing season, 1963. He is shown here with my wife, Katy. The pulling boat behind them, which we named *Java*, was built by Pete Culler. It was later replaced with the slightly shorter *Java II*. Photograph by Kinnaird Howland. (Courtesy of the photographer)

after my father's death in 1957. Herrington had learned to listen carefully to Captain Hardy when sailing plans were under discussion. He had also learned to tolerate Captain Hardy's special brand of snoring.

As guests for the first *Integrity* charter, the Colonel had invited three Cruising Club friends who had sailed with him before. Two of them were from Chesapeake Bay and one was a member of the St. Francis Yacht Club in San Francisco. I was the fourth guest, and I too had cruised with the Colonel many times before and would do so many times again. Herrington and the Howlands made a good team: he needed a cruising family and we welcomed his generous charter and his warm friendship. Having an experienced and companionable seaman like Captain Hardy aboard was not only enjoyable, but relaxing and educational for all of us.

Col. Arthur W. Herrington (1891-1970) at the wheel of *Integrity*. Unidentified photographer. (Author's collection)

One of the Colonel's party, a good inshore pilot, had on an earlier trip to Maine questioned Captain Hardy's policy for sailing to Maine, which was, in essence, "just sail east." Now the guest was our navigator, and he proceeded to compensate so exactly and completely for each change of tide and current and wind and speed that he finally got himself lost. It had been Captain Hardy's position all along that such factors generally counteracted each other. For the rest of the trip, with Captain Hardy's navigation, we easily got where we wanted to go.

Art Herrington was a very kind and hospitable man. With his memberships in the Cruising Club, the New York Yacht Club, and the Gibson Island Club, among others, he knew countless sailors, many of them prominent in the yachting world. Furthermore, as son Kin noted in the log he kept for Captain Hardy, *Integrity* herself proved to be an excellent "letter of introduction to interesting sailors everywhere she goes."

After the 1963 Cruising Club cruise ended, and before the New York Yacht Club cruise began, *Integrity* had a short provisioning layover in Camden. Arriving at the fuel dock, Captain Hardy found all spaces taken and therefore gratefully accepted the invitation of a thoughtful yachtsman to tie up alongside his boat. We went about the business of filling tanks and buying provisions while the neighboring yachtsman worked away at his chores. When the yachtsman was finished, he said, perhaps a little impatiently, that he would like to get away now. "Boy," Captain Hardy responded, "I waited twelve years for your father to get out of the White House, and now you can wait a couple of minutes for me." The yachtsman was one of Franklin D. Roosevelt's sons.

And that was not the only entertainment Captain Hardy gave us in Camden that layover. During the evening he watched a young fellow laboriously fitting screens into the companionway hatch of a nearby ketch, until he could take the sight no longer. "You don't need those screens around here," he shouted, "No Maine mosquito could get through a little hole like that."

Tom Howland, cook. Cooking aboard ship for eight or more people, three meals a day, is not easy, especially offshore and in extreme weather conditions. Tom was a master at his craft, but ultimately chose a career in maritime insurance over the lure of a Shipmate stove. Photograph by Kinnaird Howland. (Courtesy of the photographer)

The charterer for the New York Yacht Club cruise was my longtime friend John Parkinson Jr., a noted blue-water sailor and yachting historian. *Integrity* was to be the mother ship for Jack's Concordia yawl *Winnie of Bourne*. We would feed his crew, furnish bunks for some of them, and be of any help we could. Jack's wife Winnie and my wife, Katy, and I lived aboard *Integrity*, as did several of Jack's racing crew. As usual, several Concordia yawls participated in the racing, at least two of which were in home waters. We especially enjoyed visits with the John Wests, who had a summer house and a big mooring for *Gamecock* in Dark Harbor, and with the Kim Nortons, owners of *Whitecap*, who had been well entrenched at Pulpit Harbor for many years. It was a delightful ten days for all of us.

After two months and some 1,000 miles of active chartering in Maine, the slower pace of Padanaram and Buzzards Bay looked pretty good to *Integrity* and her crew. Kin took over from Captain Hardy as captain. Tom was promoted to mate. *Integrity* spent late August and early September day-sailing with special groups of passengers. Local friends were very keen to see what an oldtime schooner was really like, and we wanted to give them every opportunity to find out. We, as well as they, would be the wiser.

The first large group of guests consisted of 25 well-behaved boys and girls enrolled in the New Bedford Yacht Club sailing program. Under Captain Kin's supervision they were given a chance to experience the ship's routine. They stowed their gear below as directed. They hoisted sails in the routine prescribed

In this detail of *Integrity*'s main gaff jaws, one can see the peak halyard made off in the foreground and the lower block of the four-part throat tackle shackled to the gaff. The block under the gaff is for the topsail sheet. Photograph by Kinnaird Howland. (Courtesy of the photographer)

The aft end of the jumbo (forestaysail) boom. The jib sheet leads forward from the padeye on deck. The line on the idle ringbolt is normally fastened around the port anchor fluke. This jumbo sheet arrangement, running aloft and back down to the foremast pinrail, kept the deck clear of additional lines. The traveler obviated the need to tend the sheet while tacking. Photograph by Kinnaird Howland. (Courtesy of the photographer)

Viewed from the fore crosstrees, the eyes of the vessel are filled with essential features, including the catheads, windlass, sampson post, and bowsprit. The anchor chain flaked out on a tray has a pin inserted through a link to prevent the chain from running out prematurely. The bowsprit stays are rigged with footropes for those going forward to set or furl the jib. The staysail boom extends forward to the doubling of the bowsprit and jibboom. The staysail reef points can be seen as dark lines against the tanbarked sail. Photograph by Kinnaird Howland. (Courtesy of the photographer)

Integrity's storm anchor is fitted in deck chocks for the ocean crossing. It has a manila hawser, which provides some shock absorption in a seaway, unlike the chain of the starboard anchor. The heart-shaped flukes were designed to hang on the rail, which was protected by two half-round iron strips. Normally, the port anchor, like the starboard one, hung on the cathead. For yachts, which normally had no catheads, N.G. Herreshoff designed diamond-shaped flukes that left no shoulder to catch on an anchor's own warp. The port side of the forward hatch shows in the lower righthand corner. The after end of this rounded hatch was comfortable to sit on, kept out all unwanted water, and provided unparalleled ventilation as the wind passed over the top. Photograph by Kinnaird Howland. (Courtesy of the photographer)

order: mainsail first, foresail second, then the jib, backed to swing the bow off on the desired tack. The staysail was the last to go up, in order to leave the foredeck clear for handling anchor or mooring lines. All hands were given a chance to take the wheel and to learn that a schooner with a long keel does not handle and

Integrity taking out a class from the New Bedford Yacht Club's sailing school, 1963. The main gaff topsail has been brailed up below the main truck as the wind is rising. Photograph by Norman Fortier, neg. 16331. (Courtesy of the photographer)

respond as quickly to the rudder as does a small sloop with a tiller–that one has to think and plan ahead. They saw that *Integrity* with sails properly trimmed would hold her course steady without constant attention from the person at the helm. Captain Kin also held brief discussions about setting courses on the chart, allowing for wind and tide directions, and other problems of inshore piloting. Being on shipboard obviously made this sort of instruction more interesting and immediate to the kids than it would have been in a yacht club classroom.

With all the practicing and maneuvering, it took several hours to cross the bay to the Elizabeth Islands. Once *Integrity* was in the lee of Naushon Island, however, everyone had a chance to swim. With the schooner's low freeboard, jumping overboard was no problem and climbing back out was easy: a short ladder hung into the water about amidships, where the deck level was at its lowest. The quarterdeck and the aft deck were out of bounds for all wet bodies and dripping bathing suits. They were also out of bounds for midday sandwich and food crumbs. You see, the raised quarterdeck stopped any water on the foredeck from running aft. It just ran out the big scuppers provided for it. As Pete Culler said, proper scuppers should be at least large enough for a small cat to crawl through. A few canvas buckets of salt water over the foredecks washed any food crumbs overboard in quick order. *Integrity*'s foredecks were just made for ocean dips and picnics. The sail back to Padanaram was a fine one that afternoon. With the usual fair and fresh breeze, *Integrity* hurried along in good shape and gave her guests some happy memories.

Integrity at her mooring behind the Padanaram breakwater, with the crew preparing for a daysail. The visiting sailboat is a Beetle Cat. Photograph by Norman Fortier, neg. 14114. (Courtesy of the photographer)

Other day trips followed as weather permitted. Katy and members of her Buzzards Bay Garden Club formed the next party, and Kin provided several beach chairs on the aft deck for older members. Tom served afternoon tea via a tray set up on the aft housetop. Kin and Tom then organized day trips of all my kids' friends. During swim and lunch time, *Integrity* was not usually anchored. Instead, she was hove to, a maneuver she was very good at. On days of bright sun, the set sails automatically provided welcome areas of shade for the picnickers.

By mid-September Kin and Tom were back at school and organized sailing came to an end. Following a few family weekend cruises that fall, *Integrity* was laid up in the Concordia basin, where I could get aboard her at will. This I did quite often during the winter. There was shore power below for light, and it took just

Three working schooners in the basin at South Wharf, ca. 1965. *Integrity* is at left. The schooner in the middle was designed by Pete Culler for use on the Chesapeake. The one at right is Rose Dolan's Petersen-designed *Defiance*. Photograph by Norman Fortier, neg. 20901. (Courtesy of the photographer)

a few minutes to stoke up the wood-burning cabin heater and warm up the aft cabin. Many a friend saw and smelled the fragrant smoke floating up from the stack and requested permission to come aboard. With comfortable seats inboard of the sleeping berths, the kettle on the stove, and indirect lighting, the owner's cabin was indeed a friendly retreat for talking boats and sometimes for selling them, too.

For Christmas we dressed ship by stringing white lights from *Integrity*'s stern

rail up over both mastheads and down to the stem head. This arch of light was visible from Smith Neck Road across the harbor, from the Padanaram Bridge, and from the yacht club. I like to feel that, summer or winter, *Integrity* had become a welcome part of the life of Padanaram.

Peter Culler became *Integrity*'s professional master in 1964. Before the charter season began, we made several improvements to the ship. One, suggested by Pete, was to add some 7,500 pounds of inside ballast. For this we used granite paving blocks that weighed 25 to 30 pounds each. They were rectangular and easy to stow. They were also clean, non-rusting or corroding, and, at the time, practically free for the taking. In New Bedford at least, these blocks were often called Belgian blocks, because many of them had originally arrived in this coun-

Pete Culler at ease on the forward house, with Mate Kin Howland. Unidentified photographer. (Author's collection)

try from North Sea ports as ballast aboard ships sailing light or with no cargo. Belgian blocks could be (and in New Bedford often were) used in place of cobblestone for paving city streets. The blocks that we stowed in *Integrity*'s bilge brought her down to her lines, where she performed at her best. We seldom removed them. Just the same, it was comforting to know that they could be taken out to lighten her in case of accidental grounding or if we had occasion to carry a heavy cargo.

A second improvement was to get rid of *Integrity*'s air-cooled fisherman exhaust system that came up through the deck. I had wanted the air-cooled exhaust because it was simple. It was simple all right, and it also prevented any sea water from ever getting into the engine. In spite of the engine manufacturer's assurance that this was impossible, however, drops of oil developed on the lip of the stack and blew off from time to time, landing on the charterers' clothes. The charterers didn't like this at all. Neither did I. In 1964, therefore, we reverted to the more customary water-cooled exhaust system, after which we had no further

The author behind the wheelbox of *Integrity*, Padanaram, 1963. Photograph by Norman Fortier, neg. 14109. (Courtesy of the photographer)

problems with oil stains.

The first charter of 1964 was another cruise with Colonel Herrington to Newport. This time it was to enjoy all the activity that goes with the start of the biennial Newport-to-Bermuda Race. From our slip at Williams and Manchester shipyard we had several days to survey the racing boats and get the latest scuttlebutt. Aboard some of the boats there seemed to be an uneasy hustle and bustle to complete last-minute projects. Other boats seemed to be peacefully waiting for the start. The latter were mostly veterans of previous ocean races and would be among the prize winners. On the day of the start these same boats moved out to the starting line at a relaxed pace. When their gun went off, they moved along in fine shape.

The second charter might well have involved the Cruising Club's annual cruise, which was being held in our home waters that summer. (It had been arranged to give the returning Bermuda racers some easy sailing for a change of pace.) In fact, however, our Nonquitt friends Dick and Daisy Aldrich had chartered *Integrity* and had invited Katy and me to sail west down Long Island Sound and take in the Tall Ships festivities in New York Harbor. Dick, a former New York City councilman, was a member of the Tall Ships committee. This meant we had a front-row seat, a place in the Tall Ships parade, and invitations to all the dinners and formal occasions connected with the event.

It was all impressively different from a yacht gathering. I remember particularly the afternoon before the big ship parade. We anchored outside the Verrazano Narrows Bridge, well clear of the channel, but near enough to see several of the great ships sailing into New York Harbor. As we watched, clouds of sail suddenly appeared, ghostlike, out of the haze, soon to be joined by a huge hull coming ever closer, then sliding by so close that we could wave to the sailors arrayed on the yard. For a few magical hours, we were living in the great age of sail.

Integrity had a few days of free time after the Aldrich charter ended and before she was due in New London for the New York Yacht Club cruise. This gave Katy and me an ideal opportunity to make two brief excursions we had long planned. The first took us on a short run to Oyster Bay, Long Island, where my dear friend and great benefactor Paul Hammond had urged us to bring *Integrity* so that he could conveniently inspect her. As I have written elsewhere, I had sailed extensively with Paul on his Francis Herreshoff-designed ocean-racing ketch *Landfall* to England and on the Starling Burgess-designed schooner *Niña* to Bermuda and elsewhere. Paul was, to be sure, half a generation older than I. But in 1959-60 both of us had been dreaming about traditional workboat designs.

Captain Paul Hammond (1883-1976). Unidentified photographer. (Author's collection)

Paul was thinking about a big, shoal Thames River barge. With help from

Captain Paul Hammond's Phil Rhodes-designed, steel-hulled Thames barge yacht *Rara Avis*, built in 1959. She was designed to carry a party of six in style, with three large staterooms. Her crew numbered five: master, cook, engineer, and two deckhands. Her 10' depth of the hull provided ample headroom below, while her shallow, 4' 4" draft allowed access to many harbors that would not normally accommodate a 99' yacht. Unidentified photographer.

yacht designer Philip L. Rhodes and professional skipper Jarillo "Jay" Walter, he modified the lines and arrangements of one of these vessels, sticking with the very shoal draft (4' 4"), but changing the rig to a three-masted schooner. In 1961, he and his wife, Suzie–"The Admiral"–had taken me for a cruise on the barge in the Bahamas. *Rara Avis*, as he had named his new ship, was some 99 feet overall and 23 feet in beam, with a beautiful cabin arrangement. She was a true luxury liner of a unique type that few have ever had the chance to enjoy.

The great Estonian seaman Jay Walter was skipper aboard *Rara Avis* and had his equally gifted brother as mate. I knew them both, and they handled the big vessel beautifully in areas where the natives thought it would be impossible to enter. Jay did tell me, however, that the delivery trip from England to Nassau had been a scary one, because of the yacht's shoal draft, nearly flat bottom, and heavy, lofty rig. His account of the trip convinced me anew that it can be risky to ask a vessel to go to sea if she is not designed for such deep-water service.

Integrity had been anchored only a short time off the Seawanhaka Corinthian Yacht Club in Oyster Bay when Paul came alongside in the famous club launch *Resolute*, which is now in active service at Mystic Seaport. Crippled by failing knees, he could not climb aboard, but instead, as was his wont, had the launch make several slow turns around *Integrity*. We had a good gam, but there was not much he could say about *Integrity* except pleasantries. I have often wondered what Paul really thought about my dream boat.

Our second stop homeward-bound was at Mystic Seaport, of which I had become a member just one year previous, but where *Integrity* and her crew felt very much at home. We would have liked to stay here for a few days at least. However, we had to prepare for our charter to Percy Chubb for the New York Yacht Club cruise starting in New London on July 23. Percy was then vice commodore of the club; we were to act as mother ship for his 46-foot Sparkman & Stephens-designed ketch *Antilles*. Katy and I came along as guests, as we had done with Jack Parkinson the previous year. The cruise was in local waters: Block Island, Newport, Martha's Vineyard, Nantucket, and back. Many Concordia yawls were part of the fleet. Best of all, the Chubbs were close friends, and *Antilles* and *Integrity* were right in the middle of the action. We enjoyed ourselves hugely.

Integrity had two August charters in Maine, a third for the trip back to Padanaram, and several day charters during the *America*'s Cup races in September (one to *Newsweek* magazine). The final charter of the season was to Jack Parkinson for the fall Cruising Club rendezvous.

Some years after the 1964 *America*'s Cup races I was at the New York Yacht Club, and a friendly stranger came up to me and asked if I were Waldo Howland, owner of *Integrity*. He explained that he had been a crewman on one of the Cup sloops in 1964 and that his syndicate had rented a house overlooking Newport's entrance channel and harbor. He told me that each afternoon the crew met to review the day's racing, but that they always paused for a few minutes when the tan-barked sails of *Integrity* came into view. It was, he said, a thrill to see the old-time vessel slide gently into the anchorage, round up, and lower her sails one by one. The spirit of it was so different from his approach to racing a 12-Meter sloop, he said, yet so elemental and timeless.

Integrity started off the 1965 season with Pete Culler as captain and my oldest son, Charlie, as mate and cook. Kinny was unavailable, having signed on Drayton Cochran's schooner *Westward* for a summer passage from Athens to Bremen. In the preseason days, most of *Integrity*'s log entries dealt with "ship's work." Pete was a master at getting the schooner into top condition, cleaning on deck and below, and properly stowing all gear before doing any sailing. Thorough preparation is basic to a successful sailing season.

During some early cruising Pete and the Howlands checked out laundry, coal, ice, fuel, engine, sails. No doubt all this was a chore at times, but it had its pleasurable aspects. If you don't enjoy such chores. I suggest you think twice before you buy a boat.

Among the skills that Pete could call on was cooking. He had had plenty of experience in the galley during his many years of chartering his own ships. His culinary skills, and those of his wife, Toni, he happily shared with Charlie Howland.

There were no trips to Newport in June of 1965. Colonel Herrington was conserving his time for the three-week Cruising Club cruise to New Brunswick. I was one of his four guests for this expedition, and we shoved off just after July 4, picking up the Colonel in Scituate. We had an easy time of it on our way down the Maine coast, with stops at Biddeford Pool and Tenants Harbor. We also had plenty of fog, as usual, and took part in several Cruising Club get-togethers. Pete illustrated the ship's log with sketches of rum bottles and fog-bound buoys. I especially remember the evening when we reached Cutler. As we powered up the harbor, several local skiffs rowed out to meet us. As they came alongside, one of the young oarsmen, talking in a conspiratorial voice, said, "You look just like a pirate ship." I leaned over the rail and whispered back, "We are, but don't tell, will you?" *Integrity* had made another friend, and this made me happy.

The following night we spent in Head Harbor; then we started off in a heavy fog and a bit of old swell for St. John, New Brunswick. We were under power and all went well until midday, when we heard a horn to port. We saw no horn indicated on our chart. The only horn called for would guide us into St. John. All of our navigators were puzzled. Even with a strong fair tide, it was too early for St. John.

Pete decided to swing to port and have a look. Standing watch forward, Charlie, on the end of the bowsprit, looked down and saw birds standing on a rock, almost beneath him. The first thing I heard was breakers. At the same time I saw a steep, stony beach. Pete stopped *Integrity* immediately and swung offshore smartly, then stopped her again. One of our guest navigators, pointing his finger, said we should go that way; a second one was of a different opinion. The situation was getting awkward. At last Captain Pete said in a strong voice, "We are not going anywhere until I figure out where we are now." This is advice I have kept in mind in many situations since then, both on land and at sea.

Pete went below to the chart rack and found a chart that showed a foghorn about where he thought we were. From this known starting point we made St. John Harbor without further incident. Once we were inside, the harbormaster came alongside to show us to our berth. Here we would wait for high slack water, before proceeding over the famous reversing falls of the St. John River. Although we saw many Cruising Club boats tied up to floats, the harbormaster directed us to the big commercial dock across the way. I assume *Integrity*'s big anchor and bowsprit gear had influenced his decision.

Because of the rising tide, we had to tend our dock lines from time to time. I soon became aware of an old gentleman sitting on a box at the edge of the dock. He seemed to be interested in *Integrity*, so I climbed up the ladder to sit and pass the time of day with him. In due course I asked if he would like to come aboard and have a look around. Yes, he said, he would like that, and he descended the ladder with more agility than I had expected. After being introduced to the ship's company, he drifted over to Pete and seemed to find a kindred spirit there. As time approached for the Cruising Club to head for the falls, I asked our new friend if he would like to go up river with us as far as the Kennebekasis Yacht Club. He said, "Yes, I had planned to. My daughter is going to meet us there with the car." Good old *Integrity*, she was continuing to introduce us to interesting people.

Our new friend turned out to be a longtime St. John pilot who wanted once more to take a ship like ours over the falls and up the river. He quietly took charge, standing at Pete's elbow. Even after the leader of the CCA fleet gave the signal to proceed over the falls, our captain followed the pilot's suggestion to wait a couple of minutes more. Once through the tricky water, the pilot signed off on piloting and turned historian, giving us a running account of local lore and current facts about the territory we were passing through.

Going up the St. John River was a very different type of cruising from what I had done before. Instead of being surrounded by ever-widening waters, we found ourselves surrounded by fields, farms, and forests. There were no threatening fogs or heavy seas. However, the water was a touch thin in spots for *Integrity*'s 6′9″ draft, and the luxuriant sea grass balled up on our propeller and had to be cut away at times. A wetsuit would have been handy.

Integrity kept up well with the fleet. At Jenkin's Cove she was the center of

Cruising Club of America rendezvous, Jenkins Cove, Belle Isle Bay, New Brunswick, July 16, 1965. *Integrity*'s commodious deck could accommodate a large contingent of CCA cruisers for evening festivities. Photograph by W.T.K. (Author's collection)

activity, being able to float a most impressive crowd of congenial sailors at one time. Our final destination was Grand Lake, and it was not only a lovely place and an excellent anchorage, but its clear water was delicious to drink. Here we filled our tanks to their limits.

Back in Maine waters, *Integrity* put the Herrington party ashore at Camden and took aboard a family I did not know personally: a man and wife with two school-age sons. They arrived on time in a beautiful large sedan driven by a liveried chauffeur. It was mid-afternoon, and as soon as all their baggage was safely aboard, the man asked our steward please to bring out the cocktail tray and open the case of gin that, as his sole advance request, he had asked us to put on board. All seemed to go smoothly until, somehow, the cocktail shaker got knocked off the table. At this moment I was just leaving *Integrity* for the drive home by car. As we pulled away from the dock, I had a sinking heart. "Dear Lord," I wondered, "what have I got my friend Pete and my son Charlie into."

By phone, two weeks later, I had my answer from Charlie. This charter was absolutely perfect; the charterers were the best. They had told Captain Pete what places they hoped to visit, but let him be guided by the weather to arrange the itinerary as he thought best. The mother had told Charlie what in general the family liked to eat, but had left it up to him to supply and arrange the meals and to work with Pete on the timing. The young boys were well-behaved and helpful; they kept their gear well stowed and their cabin in perfect order. It was obvious that Pete knew Maine waters and his ship and how best to cruise in her. The charterers quickly understood how best to enjoy *Integrity* and her crew.

The next charter, also in Maine, was just as successful. The charterers were old friends of mine from New Bedford. They had done their share of schooner sailing in the past. One of their guests I also knew, but as a famous Harvard professor who taught a celebrated course in American maritime history that I had enjoyed and valued, in spite of achieving only the grade of C-. I later learned that the professor had received only a C- in boat-handling from my ship, because he had attempted (so I was told) to stop *Integrity* with the hook of his cane as Pete was bringing her alongside the dock.

Integrity had one last charter in 1965: two local couples with children, cruising in Vineyard Sound and Buzzards Bay. Then Pete stepped down as captain in early September and Kinny Howland, back from Europe and *Westward*, took his place, with my son Tom as mate and cook. They organized several cruises with school friends before the ship was laid up for the winter in the lee of South Wharf, as usual.

For the 1966 season, *Integrity* had for the first time an all-Howland crew. Kin was captain and Tom was mate and cook. (Charlie would probably have been on board also, but for the fact that he was in Somalia in the Peace Corps.) When extra help was needed for special charters, Kin signed on friends of his or Tom's.

Boat work was heavy between June 6, when Kin got out of college, and June 16, when the first charter began. It was close figuring, but at least we could haul out at Concordia Company and hence call on yard help as needed. Pete Culler was also available. Rigging, bending on sails, washing out, oiling decks, checking plumbing, servicing the engine, trying out the new hydraulic windlass–one by one the jobs got done. Kin's friend Charlie Welch, having just returned from a circumnavigation, was a great help in all the work. He stayed onboard for a few weeks as an extra hand.

On June 15, a day before the first charter formally began, Colonel Herrington, the charterer, came aboard with his two guests, Dick Randall and Captain Hardy. His first objective was Williams and Manchester in Newport. Here all hands could comfortably observe the 149 boats preparing for the Bermuda Race. I joined *Integrity* just in time for the race start. Then I sailed with her for a few more days as Art Herrington's guest.

It was on our way through Woods Hole from Buzzards Bay to Vineyard Sound that I learned an important lesson in professional seagoing etiquette. We were under power and halfway through the Hole when Captain Hardy eased over to me and asked me, as owner of *Integrity*, if he had my permission to speak to Captain Kin. I assured him that he did. Without drawing the least attention to himself, Captain Hardy then quietly told Kin that if he held his current course he would soon be aground. Kin swung the ship to the east a bit and proceeded without incident. What a wonderful man Captain Hardy really was. He saved the boat without in any way damaging Kin's reputation or self-confidence as a navigator.

During the final week in June, Colonel Herrington stayed ashore at his summer house in Quissett. While *Integrity* swung at her mooring in Padanaram, Kin and Tom went aboard *Shenandoah* as crew to pick up a few pointers from that great professional, Captain Bob Douglas, and his mates. The Colonel and his guests rejoined *Integrity* for the annual Cruising Club cruise, which was in local waters. Then Jack Parkinson was back as charterer for the New York Yacht Club cruise, also in local waters. Tom's friend Mark Pierce was now the third member of *Integrity*'s professional crew. Even for three strong and able young men, these were demanding weeks, but every day they met and dealt with wonderful people and gained valuable experience in shiphandling and in life.

Photograph by Kinnaird Howland.
(Courtesy of the photographer)

Shenandoah

Bob Douglas has been a wonderful influence on boating for many years. He designed and built this replica of a 19th-century topsail schooner at the Gamage yard in South Bristol, Maine, in 1963-64. She is outfitted with berths for 30 and operates as a cruise ship under Coast Guard provisions that the vessel has no engine. *Shenandoah* sails everywhere she goes and is handled beautifully by her owner and her crew of nine. She is a lovely sight and welcome in every port she enters.

Shenandoah was like a big sister to *Integrity* and often maneuvered to create a make-believe race between us. This both entertained guests and gave them good photo opportunities. There seems to be a natural camaraderie and good fellowship between oldtime wooden working vessels that adds something very special to sailing aboard them. They have to rely on wind, tide, and sails–and the skill and experience of their skipper–not just on the pull of the engine throttle.

On one memorable passage that Katy and I had aboard *Shenandoah*, Bob moved us from Padanaram through Quicks Hole and Vineyard Sound to Vineyard Haven almost entirely by using the tides. It was a novel and enlightening experience and gave me food for thought. Captain Robert Douglas's 109-foot topsail schooner *Shenandoah*.

For the balance of the season, *Integrity* undertook a series of short charters out of Padanaram, along with day trips for our family and friends. One of the most memorable of these was the day when we took out the local Girl Scout Mariners and their longtime leader, Louise Strongman. The captain noted in his log that they made great deckhands. They polished what brass there was. They washed down the white paint. Above all, they sailed the boat well. Rare among charterers, they left the vessel in better shape than they found her. Louise Strongman is a remarkable person. No wonder her Mariners are famous, welcome aboard wherever they go. Louise taught them not only how to sail, but, more importantly, how to live.

Integrity's time was well booked up throughout the summer of 1967 and, indeed, on through the winter to June 1968. Kin graduated from Harvard that spring and was captain. Tom was once more mate and cook. To be sure, Tom was young to be the galley chef, but he had not only had culinary experience on *Integrity*, but had also spent a summer working at the Padanaram village market and advising his customers how to cook the meat and vegetables that he sold them.

There were no significant racing events in June 1967 and, thus, no reason for an early Newport charter. This was fortunate, because special preparations were in order for the longer trips ahead. For the second time Kin hired Mark Pierce as a third member of the crew. A sailor at heart, Mark was willing to work and had great mechanical aptitude. He was soon designated bosun.

In addition to routine commissioning work, Kin added some modern equipment to *Integrity*, including a radio telephone and a depth sounder. The crew overhauled all gear and equipment, restitched sails, end-for-ended sheets, renewed worn halyards. They removed some of the stone ballast from under the cabin floorboards to make room for extra supplies. All these were tasks easier to take care of at Concordia's dock than at sea or in a foreign port. But despite the extra commissioning work, Kin was prepared to work in a few short trips and day charters.

One such assignment was for *Integrity* to add decoration and a maritime ambience to an Aldrich wedding reception. The appointed day was a fine one. The little ship was in top condition, all sails neatly flaked or furled, all flags flying in dress-ship order. From the wedding tent set up close to the beach at South Nonquitt, *Integrity* made a lovely sight, with her dark green topsides, white rail caps and houses, and tan-barked sails against a background of cloudless sky and sparkling sea. Certainly she made an ideal getaway vehicle for the departing bride and groom.

Then came our most important charter: again with Colonel Art Herrington and once more for the annual Cruising Club cruise, that year to be held in Nova Scotia. The Colonel boarded *Integrity* on July 1. By the fifth all his guests were aboard and the ship was on her way to Halifax, Nova Scotia, arriving in ample time for the Cruising Club's rendezvous on July 12. There I joined *Integrity* and enjoyed two weeks of cruising in the Bras d'Or Lakes, which just may be the loveliest cruising grounds in the world: picturesque countryside, charming, uncrowded anchorages, fair breezes, in all ways superb. No wonder the Cruising Club of America was conceived right there in Baddeck, aboard "Casey" Baldwin's 54-foot yawl *Elsie*, in sight of Alexander Graham Bell's Bras d'Or estate, Bienne Bhreagh, back in 1924.

Looking back, I recall with particular vividness the many times we rafted or anchored alongside the 40-foot aluminum Sparkman & Stephens-designed sloop *Cyane*. Her owners, Henry B. and Emily duPont, were close Chesapeake Bay friends of Art Herrington, and the leisurely cruise gave us the chance to visit and talk boats together often. I have good reason to be grateful to Colonel Herrington for introducing me to the duPonts. But more of that later.

I also vividly recall an accident that took place when Kin was bringing *Integrity* under power into a dock along its windward side. The wind was strong, the sea was bumpy, and *Integrity* swung her bow against the dock, causing a small amount of damage. A bystander on the dock, obviously a seaman, expressed a dim view of one man at the helm doing all the work while the rest of the crew looked on. And, truly, proper handling of any vessel depends on good teamwork. Ever since that morning I have, under similar conditions, tried to anticipate events and keep a proper fender close at hand. With it, I could easily have prevented or minimized that morning's damage.

Before the Cruising Club left Baddeck, the entire sailing fleet raced for the McCurdy Cup. The course was to windward up a narrow stretch of water, then back down to leeward. *Integrity* was rated the scratch boat. She finished last both on elapsed and corrected time, proving once and for all that she was not designed to win conventional races upwind. She did, however, win the hearts of local onlookers at the finish line. They waited patiently to see her finish and gave her a rousing cheer. This was welcome compensation.

The 1967 Cruising Club cruise concluded for *Integrity* in Camden, Maine. There the guests left and the crew had a few days to do catch-up ship's work and some needed provisioning. During these days *Integrity* enjoyed what Kin described in the log as a stream of interested and complimentary guests: among them the masters and crew of such cruise schooners as *Mattie*, *Mercantile*, *Stephen Taber*, *Mary Day*, and *Adventure*. She was right at home with these schooners that had been running a successful passenger business for many years. A good little wooden schooner is to me much like a piece of apple pie. The recipe was good a long time ago and will remain so for a long time to come.

Come August, *Integrity* sailed out of the past into an atmosphere of state-of-the-art yacht racing. Colonel Herrington had chartered her for some six weeks to watch the *America's* Cup trials and final match. The fact that so many of the sailors involved were Concordia clients or owners of Concordia yawls made these days especially interesting to me. Also, I had chartered our yard boat, *Fetcher II*, to the *American Eagle* Syndicate. Her short house, her shelter for the helmsman, and her long open cockpit and good diesel power made her a first-class tender for a 12-Meter sloop. With Kin running *Fetcher* at times, I felt very close to the action and to my friends J. Burr Bartram and Billy Strawbridge, who together headed the *Intrepid* syndicate. *Intrepid* eventually beat Australia's *Dame Pattie* to win the *America's* Cup.

During the *America's* Cup gathering, Percy and Corinne Chubb and I met frequently and worked out an elaborate charter for *Integrity* the coming winter. The Chubbs would leave their yawl at Concordia Company in Padanaram for some needed repairs and would loan us their professional Captain, Viv Snow, to help us sail *Integrity* down to their winter paradise on Peter Island, one of the smaller British Virgin Islands bordering the Sir Francis Drake Channel. They would let us use the big mooring in their "little harbor" and would also charter *Integrity* for several weeks. It was an exciting plan, and it was a successful one.

Kin was still in command, with Mark Pierce as mate and cook, when serious preparations began in mid-September. In addition to routine maintenance and painting, we built a hatch 18" high over the engine room: high enough to keep out deck water, but low enough to sit on, with a flush grating cover for ventilation in normal weather and a watertight cover for inclement conditions. And we had a large but simple awning made that would cover the aft deck and aft house. This was designed to set under the main boom and gaff to keep guests dry and cool.

For good ventilation below, we dreamed up a big white canvas windsail ventilator to hang between the masts and send fresh air down through the new engine room hatch. With its breeze-catching wings spread out aloft, it took an anthropomorphic form. We soon named it Mother Superior.

Amply provisioned, with new flags and charts onboard and fuel and water tanks topped off, *Integrity* was ready to sail south by the end of October. Her regular crew–Kin Howland, captain, and Mark Pierce, bosun–was augmented by Viv Snow as navigator and mate, Bob Lampson as cook and engineer, and Viv's friend Terry Burns. They made a great team. The ship departed from Padanaram on October 22 for New York and the Intracoastal Waterway. I joined the ship at Morehead City, North Carolina, for the ocean passage to St. Thomas and Peter Island.

The Virgin Islands form a part of the Leeward Islands, which extend south to the Windward Islands a distance of some 500 miles. This would be our cruising grounds for the winter. From north to south the area includes the Virgin Islands, Antigua, Guadeloupe, Martinique, St. Lucia, St. Vincent, and Grenada, just for

starters. *Integrity* was in design, construction, rig, and size very similar to many of the schooners that had been built in these waters for many years. For cargo carrying and passenger service between the islands, these vessels were well proven: handy in protected waters and reliable on rough ocean passages.

For winter cruising in the Windward and Leeward Islands, *Integrity*'s rig was particularly suitable. If we were close-hauled, we used foresail and headsails only, flattened well in, and the engine turning over at a moderate speed. With this combination we were able to hold in close to the shore and make good headway without being forced offshore into rougher water and set to leeward. We left the mainsail furled and the big awning set, which shaded passengers from the hot sun and from the brief shower that often sprang up. The awning was a blessing on a long day's sail. I have noticed time and again that too much sun can make one feel seasick as well as tired. If we were running before the wind, again we used only the big foresail and headsails. Under such conditions, the mainsail would tend to blanket the foresail and thus not be of much help. There was no need for the engine whenever the winds were favorable or fresh. And as a matter of fact they usually blew 20 mph or more.

Running before it under foresail and jumbo. According to our log, the wind was almost always easterly and fresh, 20 to 25 knots. Whether we were hard on the wind or running depended on what part of the island chain we were sailing in and whether the trade winds were blowing from the north or the south of east. With mainsail furled and awning rigged, the main boom, sail, and gaff could be raised so that there was comfortable sitting headroom beneath the awning. This would not have been possible with a fixed gooseneck arrangement. Drawing in ink by John F. Leavitt. (Author's collection)

Java II

Another very important piece of *Integrity*'s Caribbean equipment was her dinghy–or schooner yawlboat, as I prefer to think of it. The boat was designed to be rowed or sailed, to carry many people if need be, and to be short enough to hang on *Integrity*'s stern davits. The one that Pete Culler designed and built for us was traditional and perfect. With proper oars made by Culler to fit her, she was fun and efficient to row. With her little spritsail, she took no time to rig and was a joy to sail.

Cook Tom Howland (left) and bosun Mark Pierce recovering a second anchor from *Java II*, a stable little workboat. Photograph by Kinnaird Howland. (Courtesy of the photographer)

(left)
Katy and I out for an evening sail in *Java II*. Photograph by Kinnaird Howland. (Courtesy of the photographer)

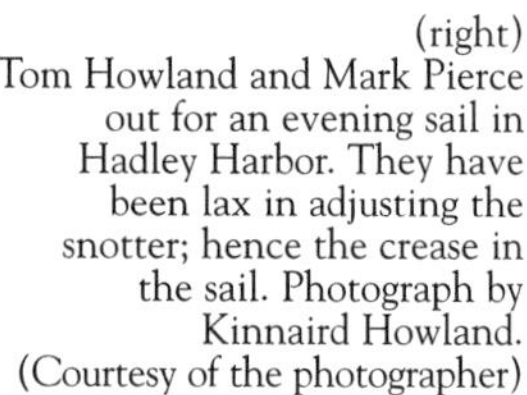

(right)
Tom Howland and Mark Pierce out for an evening sail in Hadley Harbor. They have been lax in adjusting the snotter; hence the crease in the sail. Photograph by Kinnaird Howland. (Courtesy of the photographer)

Schooner *Integrity*. Pencil drawing by William H. Ewen, Jr., of Providence, from a photograph taken by Kin Howland in October 1986 for use as a Christmas card. The tree on the foremast reflected Kin's memory of the Christmas in St. George's, Grenada, in 1967, when, following tradition, a little evergreen was lashed to *Integrity*'s fore truck. The steamboat inshore reveals artist Bill Ewen's longstanding affection for steam-powered vessels. His father played an important part in bringing the steamboat *Sabino* to Mystic Seaport. (Author's collection)

Laying to her anchor, *Integrity* was comfortable, even on a very warm day. The awning was a constant joy; Mother Superior surpassed our highest expectations. The engine room with its seats to port and starboard was a perfect location for a cool noon drink and a yarn or two. The circular white canvas body of the windsail produced a soft, indirect light from above; and the fresh air from aloft was cool and constant. Its effect was not confined to the engine room, either. A portion of it wafted out the big open galley hatch, taking the stove heat with it. Another portion was drawn forward into the fo'c'sle and out the fo'c'sle hatch. We seldom felt the need for mechanical air conditioning aboard *Integrity*. Mother Superior worked in tandem with the natural draft prevailing below decks.

When *Integrity* came to anchor or tied up to a dock, the first thing we usually did was drop the *Java*–as we called the yawlboat–into the water and tie her astern. For trips ashore to market or to pick up a visitor, we usually just rowed. For visiting another boat, *Java* was a very suitable and shipshape conveyance. No noise, no wake, no exhaust or gasoline fumes. Friends often invited us aboard. Strangers were usually happy to let us lay alongside and admire their boat and would often return the compliment.

At Fort-de-France, Martinique, I felt perfectly comfortable rowing *Java* over to the handsome 87-foot English ketch *Vanda*, flying the burgee of the Royal Ocean Racing Club. As I slowly approached, the owner came to the rail. "You must be off the green schooner yonder," he called to me. This naturally led to a pleasant chat. Leaving *Vanda*, I said that it was an unusual treat for me to meet a fellow member of the RORC. Shortly after I got back to *Integrity*, he and his wife came over for a visit. From then on, we saw a good deal of Bob and Heddy Vaughn-Jones. It turned out that they had also chartered their boat and knew all the ways of the islands. They guided and planned charter trips for us. In fact, they helped us in every possible way. Once they even took over one of our charter par-

A mighty fine crew: my sons Waldo Jr., Kin, and Tom in Carriacou. Photograph by the author.

ties, when *Integrity* was hauled out for routine maintenance.

During a layover in Antigua, I sailed *Java* out to get a closer look at the harbor entrance channel. On the way I noticed several big anchors on the beach. I studied them and wondered why they were where they were. As I was returning, the owner of a local boat beckoned me to come alongside. He then explained to me that the anchors had, in fact, been set in strategic spots so that sailing ships without power could hook onto them with long lines and warp themselves into the harbor through the channel if the wind were against them.

Almost everywhere we went our ship opened up treasure-room doors and made lasting connections for us. It is true that we lacked many luxuries that other yacht owners often find desirable. We had no power launch, no television, no running hot water, and minimal electronics. Undoubtedly a few of our guests missed these land essentials, at least for a few days. However, most of them seemed to enjoy the peace and simplicity of life aboard *Integrity*. It afforded a change from the hustle and bustle of the modern world. It allowed our guests to share in cruising life as it had been in days gone by.

While still aboard *Integrity* I had the satisfaction of delivering some hardware and other equipment to my old friend Linton "Bunny" Rigg for a native boat he was building at Tyrell Bay on Carriacou. The transaction, like my undertaking to bring supplies down for the Chubbs at Peter Island, made me feel briefly like an island trader. It seemed to add some purpose to my happy days aboard *Integrity*.

In mid-December, Katy and our three youngest children–Susie, Tom, and Waldo, Jr.–flew down to the Caribbean together for a final family cruise on *Integrity*. We lashed a small evergreen to the foremast truck and shared the twelve days of Christmas in tropical style, including joining in a series of island moonlit dance parties that began at 3:00 A.M.

Our 1968 summer charter season was more relaxed than previous ones had been, but again *Integrity* had an all-Howland crew: Kin as captain, Charlie (back from the Peace Corps) as mate, Tom as cook, and Waldo Jr. as extra crew and launchman. The ship arrived back from the Caribbean in early June. After two weeks of largely routine work, she was ready for another season, with Colonel Herrington as her first charterer and Newport and the start of another Bermuda Race her first objective.

Colonel Herrington also chartered *Integrity* for most of July, taking in the Cruising Club cruise that commenced in Block Island, then moved on to Narragansett Bay (with stops at Newport and Bristol), and so on to Buzzards Bay and local ports. *Integrity*'s charter party and crew had friends in every harbor; the yawlboat *Java* was very busy and so was Tom, the cook. Anywhere from five to ten other CCA boats were usually tied alongside for casual visits or special events. It was a lively month, but taxing on the crew.

Integrity was hauled the first week of August for bottom painting and the usual mid-season work. Then, right through Labor Day (with time out for a few one- and two-day charters) the Howlands had *Integrity* to themselves. Unlike those yacht owners who worry about children they've left behind at home, Katy and I knew where our children were: they were on board *Integrity* taking care of Katy and me.

That summer we took the Girl Scout Mariners on another day trip across the bay. This we followed with an outing for members of the New Bedford Yacht Club's sailing class, some 18 young people strong. Then came a 10-day cruise with longtime Concordia owners Bill and Katie Stetson. We decided to visit harbors where we had special friends, so that we could have them aboard for a meal or a sail. Marion, Quisset, Vineyard Haven, Edgartown, Nantucket, and Cuttyhunk were getting pretty used to *Integrity* by now.

At the end of the season, it was the children's turn to take *Integrity* on day sails or short cruises of their own. Then, as usual, *Integrity* laid up in Concordia's

South Wharf basin for the winter.

During the summer of 1968 Colonel Herrington had come up with a really challenging 12-month charter plan for *Integrity*. His primary objective was to sail to Ireland and participate in the 250th anniversary of the founding of the Royal Cork Yacht Club. As the Royal Cork Yacht Club is the world's oldest club founded specifically to "serve the interests of sailing," this could only be a historic and momentous occasion.

All of us involved with *Integrity* were immediately enthusiastic about the opportunity. We felt that *Integrity* had proved herself as a suitable ship for such a venture. On the other hand, working out a suitable crew took serious thinking.

Rex Yates and Jill Porkess, at the helm during the transatlantic passage, 1969. Photograph by Kinnaird Howland. (Courtesy of the photographer)

It was Kin who came up with the key piece to the puzzle. During his European cruise with Drayton Cochran on *Westward* in 1965 he had met Rex Yates, a young Englishman who was a fine seaman and celestial navigator. Yates was a good mechanic as well, and best of all he expressed a serious interest in becoming *Integrity*'s captain for the year-long Herrington charter. Cochran highly recommended Rex as captain. He also recommended Rex's companion, Jill Porkess, as cook. This was enough to convince me that we should sign them both up.

The one difficult decision that had to be made concerned Colonel Herrington. The North Atlantic can, as every sailor knows, be rough, even in the summer. The Colonel was 80 years old. Rex felt that it was unwise and unseamanlike to have him aboard as a crew member for the west-to-east crossing. Reluctantly, I agreed with Rex, and much as I had hoped to make the passage myself, I rearranged plans so that Art and I would fly over to Ireland and meet *Integrity* there.

Another wise decision Rex made was that he himself come aboard *Integrity* in the fall and oversee and take part in all preparations for the passage. And so *Integrity*'s cabins were made ready for Rex to live in over the winter. One of the first things he went to work on was a complete overhaul of the engine and generator. Then he did a complete rewiring job, using color-coded cable. Next, he tackled the plumbing and pumps. For each of these systems he collected all necessary spare parts and tools, as well as arranging storage spaces and tracking records for them.

I had the time and opportunity to watch Rex do much of this work and was much impressed by his thoroughness. So many boats set off on long voyages with more equipment than the crew can properly keep in good running order. As I have learned to my sorrow, any failure of preparation almost always results in eventual worry or confusion. One further example of Rex's thoroughness was his decision to take a Red Cross course and put together an extensive medical cabinet.

In early spring of 1969 Jill Porkess came aboard and immediately went to work. First she checked out *Integrity*'s galley equipment and added to it items that she had found useful or necessary on other vessels. Next she went about organizing the storage and working areas with a particular view to safety and convenience. In her planning she consulted with Tom and other Howlands who had spent time in the galley. By cooking and living aboard during these spring weeks, she got her routines worked out and was well prepared for the voyage. Feeding seven hungry crew members for many weeks at sea is a demanding job. Jill was ready for it. To help her with her task, we fitted the Shipmate stove with an oil burner, which allowed the cook to turn off the stove when it wasn't needed. This would have been impossible using coal. It also allowed us to tap the engine fuel line and eliminate the heavy and dusty coal bin.

Rex had help in the regular spring commissioning from the crew-to-be. In addition to Charlie, Kin, and Mark Pierce, Rex's friend Caes De Grass, and a young man from Padanaram, Anthony "Chuck" Foster, joined in the work to learn the ways of *Integrity*. This group made a good crew of seven, which was the right number for an ocean passage in the schooner. Everyone had their own berth. This left the transom berth alongside the cabin table always available at mealtime and for other uses.

Integrity departed for Ireland on the same day that 24 boats started the 1969 Transatlantic Race. I was very sorry to have missed the ocean passage, which

Charlie and Kin assured me went well, except for some minor chafe caused by the foresail gaff jaws. (This was corrected with metal sheathing easily installed by climbing the ratlines in the fore rigging.) On the whole the weather was good.

Integrity's European crew, 1969. Front (left to right): Caes De Grass; Captain Rex Yates; Colonel Arthur W. Herrington; Mate Kin Howland; Charlie Howland. Back (left to right): Anthony Foster; bosun Mark Pierce; cook Jill Porkess. Photograph by Norman Fortier, neg. 17466. (Courtesy of the photographer)

For the two days that they experienced gale-force winds, the crew stowed the mainsail, reefed the foresail and forestaysail, and hove to. With the foresail sheeted fairly flat and the forestaysail slightly backed, *Integrity* moved ahead very slowly and had no tendency to fall off or come up into the wind. This is just what a good schooner is supposed to do. Charlie said that on deck the wind screamed through the rigging and the seas were threatening. Below, however, the motion was not bad at all; conditions were surprisingly quiet. It is a comforting feeling to know that your ship will take care of herself in a breeze of wind, if you treat her right.

The Colonel and I flew into Ireland on the Fourth of July. In Dublin we had temporary quarters at the Blarney Hotel. The cabbie who drove us to Dublin was named Eddie, and we had hired him for the day. As it turned out, he stayed with us for more than a week, and we had the good fortune to see more of southern Ireland and its people than would otherwise have been possible.

We caught up with *Integrity* in Cork Harbor on July 5. Believe me, she was a welcome sight. When we went aboard, we found all the crew in great shape. The Howlands had gained weight and grown an interesting assortment of beards. Lunch was about to be served. It included cold beer from the ship's icebox and freshly baked bread and cookies from the ship's stove. *Integrity* herself not only looked to be in beautiful shape above and below decks, she smelled good, too. Although the first yacht to finish the race to Ireland had taken only 11 days and *Integrity* had taken 21 days, I nevertheless felt proud of her showing. You see, she was already in shape to continue her work, whereas the fast boats had to spend some days in a boatyard before being ready to go again.

Between the hospitality shown us by members of the Royal Cork Yacht Club and the many interesting boats that were in Cork Harbor for the celebration, time sped by. "My father did get a chance to kiss the Blarney Stone," Kin noted in the log, "but not the redhead who served the paddy."

Before I left for home on July 9, I had the opportunity to stop in Arklow, home of the Tyrell family, famous for generations as builders of fine wooden vessels. My old friend Major Smyth had often spoken to me about the Tyrell boatyard. Getting to see it at last was a pleasure and an education that I'll never forget. It was still very much a family operation. John Tyrell spent several hours with me–he said he enjoyed talking with "a man of the same cloth." For the first time I saw logs so big and heavy that they were sawn on the ground with a movable saw on tracks cutting through them. That summer I had a potential buyer for a big schooner and would certainly have wanted John to build her. He said there was nothing he would rather do than build one last wooden ship. My customer had the money. He had paid us for drawing up plans. Alas, he was lost during a storm in a small plane headed for St. Thomas.

After several of our young crew and I had left for home, *Integrity* gave Colonel Herrington and his guests an unbelievably busy and varied summer. The big day for the Royal Cork Yacht Club's 250th anniversary was July 13. Boats from the CCA and the Royal Cruising Club joined the Cork fleet for a dress-ship parade starting and finishing in Cork Harbor. A majority of the yachts, including *Integrity*, then went on a "go as you please" 12-day cruise around the southern coast of Ireland. From Ireland, *Integrity* went on to England and the Cowes Week regatta, which was followed by the annual rendezvous of the RCC on the Beaulieu River, at which Colonel Herrington and his party were guests of Commodore Swann. Then it was over to Lisbon, Portugal, with Commodore R.S. Berridge of the Irish Cruising Club as one of the Colonel's guests.

Integrity remained in Lisbon for several weeks. Katy and I came back aboard for ten days, during which I spoke with two different yachtsmen who had a serious interest in buying the schooner. The talks did not produce results. However, Colonel Herrington's friend Count De Correia entertained us royally, both on his yacht and at his home. It was indeed a grand visit.

With the coming of fall and a long-range forecast for favorable weather conditions for an Atlantic crossing to the West Indies, Alan Bemis, the newly elected commodore of the CCA, and his two-man guest crew joined Colonel Herrington for the voyage to Grenada. These three added to *Integrity*'s three professionals, and the Colonel, brought the crew complement up to seven, the previously determined limit for a long passage in the ship. Once again I reluctantly stepped aside.

Integrity under reefed mainsail, full foresail, and forestaysail (jumbo). This is the rig we used constantly sailing the Southern Route back to the Caribbean. With the trade winds it gave us enough sail to make good progress even with the wind well aft. All sails stayed full, and with the jumbo fairly flat the ship had no tendency to come up into the wind and kept nicely to her course. Drawing in ink by John F. Leavitt. (Author's collection)

However, the situation changed before long. The first leg of the crossing was discouragingly slow for lack of wind. Alan Bemis and one of his guests had to leave *Integrity* in Cape Verde to be sure of getting home in time for Christmas. This was a disappointment for them. For me it resulted in a welcome telegram requesting that I join the ship as soon as possible, which I did. Joel White was Alan Bemis's third guest, who, to my delight, had decided to stay with *Integrity*.

Thus we got to know each other as shipmates, having already met as fellow boatyard operators. Joel and I would have other happy meetings in the future, too, as you will learn.

From the Cape Verde Islands to Grenada we had fair weather and good and fair winds, and we made good time. With the mainsail reefed, the big foresail always stayed full and pulled us along well even with the wind dead aft. Steering was a delight. So was the motion of the ship.

As rigged, *Integrity* proved to be a fine passage-maker and easy on her crew. Bosun Pierce served tea every afternoon on a tray set crosswise on the aft end of the aft house. With the spout of the teapot facing to leeward and the pot itself carefully placed, it poured on its own. This was on the roll down. On the roll back the flow stopped automatically. Pierce replaced the full mug with an empty one, and so all the tea was poured in proper seagoing fashion. This demonstration of virtuosity at teatime earned Mark the sobriquet of "Mrs. Pierce," in addition to his formal rank of bosun. We were not really roughing it on *Integrity*, that's for sure.

Comparing notes in Grenada with Jack Parkinson and Drayton Cochran, who had begun their passage from Lisbon at about the same time we did, we learned that our time across was almost as fast as theirs. This we achieved without troublesome spinnaker drills, for the simple reason that we carried no spinnaker. Neither did we eat off the same soggy paper plates two or three times. Aboard *Integrity*, we dined on clean china.

Integrity slid silently into Grenada's little inner harbor of St. George's on Christmas Eve 1969. The sun had just dropped below the western horizon and harbor lights were appearing all around us. Friendly people aboard anchored boats welcomed us with messages of good cheer. It was indeed an auspicious start for another winter season in the Caribbean.

In early January, Alan and Chapie Bemis, along with the artist Dwight Shepler and his wife, flew down to Grenada, and I joined them for a two-week cruise aboard the Vaughn-Jones's *Vanda*. I had to substitute this lovely ketch for *Integrity*, which was still up on the railway. It turned out to be a doubly fortuitous arrangement. We had a wonderful cruise guided by a skipper who was very familiar with the Grenadines, and the Bemises went on to charter *Vanda* for the following year's CCA winter cruise.

At the end of March, Colonel Herrington came back aboard for the return trip to Padanaram, with Captain Rex Yates still in charge. Rex and Jill had certainly done a marvelous job with *Integrity*: a full year's charter, over 15,000 miles of cruising to Europe and back, three months in the Caribbean, and, finally, home without a single mishap that I know of or any delays, except those caused by lack of wind: a truly remarkable record. As for *Integrity* herself, she seemed to be up to any task she was asked to perform.

Although I formally put *Integrity* up for sale in the summer of 1970, the Colonel continued his charter for local sailing and for the local CCA cruise in July. As you can well imagine, it was a wrench to sell *Integrity* after all she had done for the Howlands. The temptation to keep her was tremendous. But times do change. My boys were all busy now and beginning careers of their own. My brother and I had sold our boatyard, Concordia Company, Inc. Katy and I had a busy retirement to look forward to. During the fall, three yachtsmen bought *Integrity* in partnership. That same fall my dear friend and *Integrity*'s great patron, Colonel Art Herrington, died. An era had ended.

Integrity in between charters, Padanaram Harbor, 1970. Photograph by Norman Fortier, neg. 14108. (Courtesy of the photographer)

In November 1970, under a new professional crew, *Integrity* left Morehead City for a winter of cruising in the West Indies. A few days after her departure I received a most upsetting phone call from one of the new owners. He told me that *Integrity* had run into some bad weather and had been rolled down by two rogue waves. She had received some damage. The crew felt it was imperative to abandon ship in favor of a rescue by a passing freighter.

The full story of *Integrity*'s abandonment, salvage, and eventual sinking has been ably told by the English sailor and writer Frank Mulville in his book *Schooner Integrity* (London, 1979; also published in the U.S. under the title *Death of the Schooner Integrity*, Boston, 1981). It is a tale of five years of confusion, mystery, intrigue, and neglect.

I prefer to recall happier days with *Integrity*. She meant a great deal to all of us who sailed on her. She continues to sail on in our memories.

At this stage in my life, as I become more and more timid, I can hardly believe I ever had the courage to undertake the building of a seagoing vessel, much less the ability to charter her successfully for a decade. It seems that there is a time for almost everything–and that you must not waste it when it comes.

I have asked myself how my dream could have worked out so well. Even now I cannot visualize any other type of boat that would better have accomplished all that I had in mind or would have done it more economically. Would a well-conceived powerboat have done as well? For someone else, perhaps. But such a boat would have been out of the question for me. In any case, a lack of fuel capacity for long voyages would likely have ruled out that option.

In fact, *Integrity* was a proven sailing type that had been thoroughly tested and perfected by small crews over many years. Her wooden sawn-frame construction is still one of the best ever devised. It is understood the world over and in most cases is practical for builders using local woods and available tools. *Integrity* proved to be comfortable to sail and live aboard for both short and long periods. In discussing the various *Integrity* charters, I have tried to suggest her many good qualities and features. I have also tried to indicate the importance of the character of those who chartered and sailed her: their experience, their attitude, their understanding. And I mustn't forget that *Integrity* had a supportive home port and a boatyard of her own.

My experience with *Integrity* led me inevitably towards a close association with Mystic Seaport, which faithfully keeps alive so many of the essential verities of traditional seafaring and preserves good, authentic examples of good proven boat types and designs. In this respect, too, *Integrity* has continued to reward me in ways past counting.

Part II:

Mystic Seaport

On the present site of Mystic Seaport's Henry B. duPont Preservation Shipyard, the shipyard operated by Charles Mallory and his sons was just south of the Greenman yard. Here the pilot schooner *Telegram* is on the ways in preparation for her launch in December 1875. The large mold loft building behind the schooner had bays for lumber storage on the ground floor. What appears to be an open-ended sawmill stands at right. The site was originally occupied by Peter Forsyth about 1846, and the Mallorys leased the yard from 1851 to 1883, launching 59 vessels, including 7 clipper ships, and 33 wooden screw steamers. Photograph by Edwin A. Scholfield. (Mystic Seaport 1965.859.5)

5
Starting Out at Mystic Seaport

In 1963 Mystic Seaport trustees J. Burr Bartram and John Parkinson Jr., both close sailing friends of mine, persuaded Katy to make our family members of Mystic Seaport. It was another two years, however, before Waldo Jr. and I drove down to Mystic to see what it was all about. On that fall visit I initiated what was to become a routine stop at the administration building to speak to the director–at that time Waldo C.M. Johnston. Waldo Johnston himself was a newcomer to the Museum. He greeted us as one Waldo would be bound to greet two other Waldos–most cordially. He suggested that Waldo Jr. and I take a leisurely look around, then come back and have lunch with him.

The location and layout of Mystic Seaport struck me as charming, unique, and full of promise. The low point of land on which it was situated had been partially filled and confined within wooden bulkheads. An interesting collection of small historic buildings lined the shore. Historic ships large and small were on exhibit, some on land, some in the water. And my old friend, the whaleship *Charles W. Morgan*, was much in evidence, secured in riprap, sand, and gravel more or less as she had been when I last saw her in 1937 at Round Hill in Dartmouth, Massachusetts.

The Museum lays on the east side of the Mystic River—a tidal estuary—about three miles above its mouth and about half a mile upstream from downtown Mystic.

Across from the Museum's waterfront, the west shore of the Mystic River is still lined with 19th-century mariners' homes and is relatively undeveloped because the wide flats prevent dockage on along much of that side of the river. Much of the east shore already belonged to the Museum and looked like a true

Topsides of *Charles W. Morgan* being rebuilt with help from outside contractors, November 1950. Because she lay in a sand berth, her bottom could not be properly repaired. Unidentified photographer. (Mystic Seaport 1950-8-53)

In this ca. 1875 view up the Mystic River, the future site of Mystic Seaport fills the background. At left, the mold loft and sawmill chimney of the George Greenman & Company shipyard occupy the point where museum exhibits are located today. At far right, the Mallory shipyard stands partially on the site site of the future Mystic Seaport shipyard. The church and houses are now part of the Museum as well. The wooden steamship *Aurora* was launched at the Mallory yard in 1874. Photograph by E.A. Scholfield. (Mystic Seaport 1965.859.10)

19th-century seaport. Except for a narrow channel near the east shore, the water was perfect for small-boat rowing and sailing, but, fortunately, too shoal for moorings and a fleet of private pleasure boats. Upriver were picturesque marshes and shallow waters, with a quiet old cemetery on the east side of the river. Still further north, at a distance, was the newly completed Route I-95, the major interstate highway joining New York with Providence and Boston. Travelers had, from a high scenic vantage stop, a beautiful view of Mystic Seaport, but automobiles were too far away for traffic noise to disturb the Museum's peace. Downriver to the south, at some little distance was the highway drawbridge crossed by U.S. Route 1 and then the railway swing bridge and higher land, all protecting the Museum basin from seasonal storms. Equally approachable by land or sea, it was an absolute jewel of a location. Only the good Lord could have designed such an ideal setting for a seaport museum.

At lunch Waldo wanted to know what I thought of it all, and I allowed that the project seemed to me unbelievably exciting and worthwhile. But I could not refrain from adding that the ship and small craft exhibits looked awful–truly awful–and were in woeful condition.

No doubt I should have been less blunt, but my immediate enthusiasm for Mystic Seaport and my shock at the appearance of the boats were too great for me to soften my conclusions. I doubt that Waldo Johnston felt that conditions were as bad as I had painted them. Nevertheless, the prospect of all Mystic's ships and small craft rotting away in a few years was sobering for both of us.

After lunch I asked Waldo where I would find John Leavitt's office. I had heard that John was at the Museum now, and I had not seen him since the 1930s, when we worked together in a yacht brokerage office on State Street in Boston. John and I had a very enlightening conversation that afternoon, one that I vividly recall even now.

John F. Leavitt (1905-74) was born in Lynn, Massachusetts, but spent his late teens and early twenties working on coasting schooners along the Maine coast. He then worked as a yacht skipper, a rigger, a journalist in Lynn and Marblehead, and for 20 years as a yacht broker. During that time he also became an accomplished marine painter. He joined the staff at Mystic Seaport in 1960 and was shipkeeper on the *Charles W. Morgan* when I first visited. Later, as associate curator, he was the Museum's leading expert on working sail. His charming book, *Wake of the Coasters*, was published in 1970. Unidentified photographer. (Mystic Seaport 1962-2-9)

First, John briefly brought me up to date on his own history. He told me that he had come to Mystic Seaport in 1960 as shipkeeper for the *Charles W. Morgan.* His version of the Museum's early history was that a group of dedicated marine-oriented benefactors had, in 1929, dreamed up a bold and farsighted plan for a maritime historical society and museum. They had picked out an exceptionally fine location for their purposes and in subsequent years had collected many excellent historic artifacts that would have been lost to posterity, if it had not been for their efforts and foresight. Then John told me about a crisis that the Museum had suffered soon after he joined the staff. His account squared with one that my friend Tom Hale, an early Mystic Seaport staff member, had given me some years before about the same museum crisis.

As Mystic Seaport had grown in size, the founders had gradually added to the staff a number of seriously interested young professionals who wished to make their life's work at a great maritime museum. Tom was one of these young professionals. He had moved to Mystic Seaport from Marblehead and had invested in a new house for his family in Noank. Tom worked with enthusiasm at the Museum. All too soon, however, the Museum's ambitious institutional goals and its limited financial resources led to conflict. Rather than historical accuracy and authenticity, entertainment and expediency seemed the surest path to increased visitorship and income. This trend disillusioned and discouraged Tom and the other young professionals. Most of them resigned–a loss for them personally and for the Museum as well.

John Leavitt had been in complete sympathy with Tom's group, but he did not resign. His situation was quite different from theirs. Because he was an experienced seaman, his assignment at the time had been straightforward maintenance onboard the *Morgan*. Nonetheless, John too had had problems. From the start he realized that the *Morgan* and the other vessels were in perilous condition, and he had pleaded with management for a larger crew and more facilities to help get these exhibits in order. Despite his experience, his pleas were receiving very little attention. To put it mildly, he himself was becoming very discouraged.

As son Waldo and I drove back to Padanaram from that first visit, my thoughts were sober but hopeful. Staff morale and physical conditions were at a low ebb. With a bit of time, however, and some concerted effort (and, of course, the willing dollar), I believed that things could be changed for the better.

Back at Concordia Company during that same fall of 1965, I talked with Pete Culler and Martin Jackson about the condition of the Museum's watercraft collection. The small boats displayed outside were drying out, looked very shabby, and begged for attention. The larger craft that had come to Mystic in poor condition in the first place were now literally rotting away. What could be done?

All three of us agreed that taking the craft to private boatyards for rebuilding or maintaining would be too expensive. Furthermore, these yards were not really set up with the special skills and materials needed by Mystic Seaport's fleet. The Museum unquestionably had to have a shipyard of its own if it hoped to have an enduring fleet of historic vessels.

My good friend Major William Smyth and I spent many hours discussing the fleet of ships at Mystic Seaport. Here in the hold of the *Charles W. Morgan*, we inspect her condition. As described in the earlier volumes of this work, Major Smith grew up in Fairhaven, Massachusetts, and worked there at the Peirce and Kilburn Shipyard before moving to Mystic Shipyard in 1938. We had been longtime sailing companions and friends, and I greatly valued his insight as a member of the Museum's Ships Committee.
Photograph by Lester Olin. (Mystic Seaport 1971-6-275 T)

Once more in 1965 I drove back to Mystic to consult with my mentor and close friend Major Smyth, who was now one of the owners of the downriver Mystic Shipyard. A Mystic Seaport enthusiast, he was living in nearby Noank, and he and his wife always had a meal for me, and often a bunk, too, so that I could stay overnight. On this particular visit, sitting comfortably in front of his open fireplace, we had a long discussion about the prospects for a functioning shipyard at Mystic Seaport. It was all on the positive side. When I left early the next morning with a good breakfast under my belt, I had a better sense of just what the Museum would have to do–and I shared my thoughts that same morning with Waldo Johnston.

Although Waldo felt that the undertaking might be too ambitious, he promised to consider it. The following summer, while cruising in Maine aboard his yawl *Natty Bumpo III*, he had a timely and important gam with Henry Scheel, a well-known Mystic area resident, yacht designer, and Mystic Seaport trustee, who was also cruising Down East on his sloop *Pride and Joy*. Between them, in this relaxed atmosphere, they began organizing a ships committee to consider solutions for the Museum's critical boat repair and maintenance problems.

The year 1966 turned out to be a time of reassessment at Mystic Seaport and of many staff resignations. It was also the year that Francis Day Rogers became the new board president. What a wonderful president he proved to be! That fall the Ships Committee finally came into being. Rogers appointed Henry Scheel chairman; Waldo Johnston was, of course, a charter member; and I also joined the committee, along with several trustees.

It didn't take many formal meetings for the Ships Committee to reach some specific conclusions: Mystic Seaport's fleet was in bad condition; its current crew of five or six repair specialists could not make even a dent in the backlog of ships' maintenance work; and the outside display of small craft was a sorry show. True, a few boats had been or were still being sent out to private yards for rebuilding. But not only was such work costly, it was work that should have been observable as part of the museum experience for visitors.

In 1957 the Museum installed its Firefly marine railway on the point where the George Greenman & Company shipyard had stood. In this view the 18' cutter *Galena* (ex-*Fox*, ex-*Cockle*) is hauled on the railway shortly after being added to the Museum's collection. Designed by James Purdon and built by Graves at Marblehead, this deep-draft, English-style cutter was once owned by the noted yacht designer W. Starling Burgess, whose son Frederic sailed her at Provincetown in the 1920s. Unidentified photographer. (Mystic Seaport 1957-8-50)

In 1960, some six years previous, the 78-year-old iron training ship *Joseph Conrad* had been towed to New London's Thames Shipyard for an experimental coating of sprayed-on fiberglass over her deteriorating bottom plating. In the 1950s, the whaleship *Charles W. Morgan*, then nearly 110 years old, had had her topsides replaced while she lay in her bed of sand. It evidently did not turn out to be a durable repair.

From the beginning, my main objective at Ships Committee meetings was just to keep hammering away at the absolute necessity for a shipyard at the Museum, one that would eventually include a crew of 30 to 34 people. We all agreed that a main shipyard building should be big enough to house any one of our three largest vessels. We also felt that a lift dock would be the most suitable facility for our hauling needs. It would take up less space than a big railway and cost less than a dry dock. For medium-sized floating craft, we already had a useable small railway on Lighthouse Point.

I was invited to attend the first trustees' meeting that would consider the shipyard project–and to present the position of the Ships Committee on the subject. Frankly, I found it a bit daunting to stand before this august gathering, but I did already know quite a few of them; the others were obviously interested in what I had to say.

Mr. and Mrs. Alfred Ogden in front of their lovely country house in Stonington, Connecticut, at about the time of my first visit with them. Unidentified photographer. (Courtesy of Alfred Ogden)

The trustees countered my presentation with all the practical reasons why we couldn't afford a shipyard. And I in turn responded that, if this was actually the case, we could forget having a fleet at Mystic Seaport. Ships, I explained, are not at all like monuments in brick or stone that one creates and enjoys for years to come with only minimal care. They are, in fact, much more like human babies and need daily love and attention.

Despite the quite negative response of some board members, it was clear that the trustees had taken the report of the Ships Committee seriously. The board instructed me to talk to the chairman of the Museum's Planning Committee about the feasibility of a shipyard. The chairman was Alfred Ogden, a highly respected New York lawyer. I made an appointment to meet him a few Sundays later at his country house in Stonington.

After a delightful lunch, Alfred and I spent most of that Sunday afternoon walking around the Museum waterfront. Alfred allowed that he was not wholly familiar with boats and their maintenance problems. Looking closely at a few of the small craft, he could see that sun and rain were wreaking havoc. Going below on one of the larger ships in the water, it was easy to identify the leaks, the mildew, the rotting

Mr. and Mrs. Clifford B. Mallory Jr. Two wonderful people, Cliff and Pauline seem to me to represent the very best values and traditions of Mystic Seaport. Descended from Charles Mallory, who settled as a young sailmaker in Mystic in 1816 and eventually prospered as a shipowner and shipbuilder, Clifford maintained the family tradition of service to Mystic Seaport established by his father in the 1930s. He met and married Pauline, a charming New Zealander, during his U.S. Navy service in World War II. The Mallory family's shipping interests are depicted in the Mallory Building exhibit at the Museum. Unidentified photographer. (Author's collection)

Pete Culler and I discuss the *Charles W. Morgan* before a meeting of the Ship's Committee, October 25, 1973. Photograph by Mary Anne Stets. (Mystic Seaport 1973-10-94D)

wood. We could both feel and smell the unhealthy condition of things. Nevertheless, it was difficult for Alfred to understand my assertion that Mystic's fleet required daily attention.

"Do you really mean what you are telling me?" he asked. I could answer with complete confidence that, yes, I had spent my whole life thus far amidst wooden boats and was fully conversant with their needs. Boats being worked in their trade, I pointed out, automatically receive timely attention; topsides and decks are constantly splashed, cleaned, and pickled in salt water; rigging is renewed as necessary; bilges get pumped regularly; sails get dried. These Museum boats, on the other hand, just sit and suffer.

To his immense credit, Alfred stopped and reconsidered the situation. "I do believe you," he said finally, "and we will have to figure out what is to be done." From that day forward Alfred cooperated wholeheartedly with the efforts of the Ships Committee, becoming an essential part of our team. Work on the new shipyard had begun.

As the months went by the Ships Committee slowly grew and it held meetings more regularly. Gradually, a few members who could easily get together became part of an informal subcommittee that could discuss and act upon day to day matters. Major Smyth and I were part of that group. So was Pete Culler (generally in absentia). Don Robinson of the Museum's administrative office became more involved. Others helped as circumstances warranted.

In 1970 I was elected a Museum trustee and appointed Chairman of the Ships Committee, replacing Henry Scheel who had moved to Maine. At one of the earliest board meetings I attended as a member, we discussed the financing of a Museum shipyard: how much would be needed, where the money would come from. As I passed trustee Clifford Mallory Jr. on the way out of the meeting, he winked at me and drew me to him. "Don't you worry, Waldo," he said, "we'll find the money." This was encouragement indeed, and a sharper picture of the Ships Committee's methods and purposes developed in my mind. Gradually, a few members who could easily and frequently get together became an informal subcommittee that could discuss and act upon day-to-day matters. Major Smyth, shipyard supervisor Maynard Bray, and I were part of that group. So were John

Leavitt, Waldo Johnston, and Don Robinson (the Museum's boat-minded associate director). Others helped as circumstances warranted.

Our subcommittee would carefully study and amplify shipyard objectives and challenges. We would make up a detailed agenda for our regular meetings of the full Ships Committee, the expanded membership of which included such boat-oriented trustees as Olin J. Stephens II, yacht designer and ocean racer par excellence, and Captain Irving Johnson, celebrated around-the-world sailorman. We sought to keep these trustees closely informed of our ship and boat related activities and prospects–and get their active advice, suggestions, and supports. In this way the full Ships Committee, voting in unison, would carry maximum weight during board meetings–and elsewhere, for that matter.

To put it another way, we aimed to present carefully thought-out solutions, rather than briefly considered suggestions. This method could and often did save valuable trustee and staff time and let us get on with other business at hand. Slowly but surely a good system for ship maintenance was evolving.

Shipyard Supervisor Maynard Bray makes a point about the *Charles W. Morgan* to Major Smyth and me. Commencing in the Spring of 1969, real progress on a ships maintenance program began to take shape. Waldo Johnston, went on an early season mission to England and Scandinavia to visit several maritime museums. His main purpose was to observe the ship preservation techniques that were being followed in those parts of the world. It was April 1st when Maynard Bray was hired to be the superintendent of a growing boat maintenance workforce. This was no April Fool appointment, I can tell you; it was one of the best decisions that the Museum could have made. In due course it was to greatly benefit maritime history in general, Mystic Seaport and me in particular. Almost immediately Mystic's small craft began to receive the attention they had been needing for so many years. Photograph by Mary Anne Stets. (Mystic Seaport 1973-10-9A)

In the spring of 1969 Waldo Johnston went on a mission to England and Scandinavia to visit several important maritime museums. His main purpose was to observe the ship preservation techniques and standards that prevailed in those parts of the world. Then, on April 1st, Maynard Bray was hired by Curator Ed Lynch to superintend Mystic Seaport's growing boat maintenance work force. This was no April Fool appointment, I can assure you; indeed, it was one of the best decisions that the Museum could have made. Over the years it has been proven a great benefit not merely to Mystic Seaport or me personally, but to the cause of maritime preservation and history in general.

Almost immediately Mystic Seaport's small craft began to receive the attention they had been needing for so many years. A spar shed was converted into a covered small craft exhibit space. The spars themselves were easily sheltered under an attached lean-to. Smaller boats and dinghies found a home in a metal building up on the hill on the inland side of Greenmanville Avenue. Here they were at least secure and protected from the weather, even if not accessible to visitors. The few boats temporarily stored outside were protected by new canvas covers. Several small craft were sent to good private yards for restoration, such as Crosby's in Osterville.

The Museum's big vessels also received additional attention in 1969. The *Charles W. Morgan* was a particularly sad sight and poor exhibit at that time. Squatting in her bed of sand and partially down-rigged, she reminded me of a broody hen or an overripe melon; such was the bulging of the lower area of her topsides. Unless my memory is running away with me, wooden shingles had been pounded into her widest seams. As soon as the growing work force could get to them, the *Morgan*'s topsides were properly refastened and her lower deck was rebuilt to tie the hull together properly. The *Morgan* sat tall again and revealed her proper lines. If only her bottom had not still been imprisoned in the sand.

By the spring of 1970 the trustees were, I believe, thoroughly aware that a full shipyard, complete with lift dock, was an absolute necessity for an enduring Mystic Seaport, and they officially approved this objective at a board meeting held in September. Only the money for building such a shipyard was now lacking. At this critical moment, Clifford Mallory's whispered prophecy came true. With a carefully drawn budget and prospectus to study and consider, the family of Henry B. duPont agreed to underwrite the shipyard with a most generous and timely contribution. The new facility would be named The Henry B. duPont Preservation Shipyard in memory of a very special former trustee, who, with his wife, Emily (who had succeeded Henry as a current trustee), had already done so much for Mystic Seaport.

This was a major turning point for the Museum. The promise of a living fleet was now in sight rather than merely a dream in the offing, and now the actual process of creating the shipyard could get underway. Maynard Bray was put in charge of the project. He soon made the splendid decision to hire Gene Baudro as his assistant and second in command. Gene was a young independent contractor who lived in the nearby town of Ledyard. He not only knew his own trade thoroughly; he knew where to find local services and supplies. He was a tremendous asset to the shipyard from its inception to its completion.

It had already been agreed that the site of the new shipyard should be on the south end of the Museum property, where there was ample space and relatively deep water just off the shore. Indeed, this was approximately the site of the shipyard where Clifford Mallory's great-grandfather Charles Mallory had built seven clipper ships in the 1850s. As for the design of the main shipyard building, several alternatives were proposed at trustee meetings. One group thought it would be best to seek out a suitable old building, move it piece-by-piece to Mystic, then reassemble it on the grounds. Others urged the Museum to hire an architect to draw up plans for a structure that could then be built from scratch.

Meanwhile, our Ships Committee was working on a more traditional approach. Following the thinking of shipyard owners of the past, we felt that, first of all, the Ships Committee would know better than anyone else what was needed and how to achieve it. We reasoned that our shipyard crew should and would be building and equipping this facility–and, most important of all, using it on a daily basis. In other words, we believed we should be our own architects and in charge of our own planning and building.

I did fear that such thinking might strike the board and administration as presumptuous and high-handed. It was not the usual thing for a Mystic Seaport department to proceed too far on a project before gaining approval from the board. However, I had a theory of museum development I wanted to push, and the shipyard seemed like a grand first opportunity for pushing it. I called my

In this aerial view from May 1970, the filled land on which the Shipyard would be located shows prominently at lower right. Photograph by Russell A. Fowler. (Mystic Seaport 1970-5-257)

approach the "Do-It-Yourself" theory. At least, I figured, you should use your own best judgment first, and use your own crew as much as possible, before calling in outside experts and contractors and promoters. Outside consultants tend, quite understandably, to push their own plans and initiatives without necessarily understanding an institution's culture and long-range plans. In any event, the Ships Committee did proceed to test the Do-It-Yourself theory.

With the site settled upon, the next move was to prepare plans for the shipyard's main shop building. Because I had experience building a comparable shed at Concordia Company some years before, Maynard Bray and I drove over to South Dartmouth to look over the shed where Leo Telesmanick and his crew were building Beetle Cats for Concordia–and see if its design could be modified for use at the Museum. First we took a number of basic measurements for future reference. Then we figured how long, how wide, and how high the Mystic shed would have to be to accommodate any one of our three biggest ships, the *Charles W. Morgan*, the fishing schooner *L.A. Dunton*, and the training ship *Joseph Conrad*.

These calculations were relatively easy. As I recall, Maynard scaled off the shed perimeters on a opened-out brown paper bag. The pitch of the roof was held to the angle that carpenter Wilton Gifford had told me was best for New England houses and other buildings. Go along horizontally 12 inches, he said, then up vertically about eight inches, and the third side of this triangle would be the correct pitch, steep enough to shed water and snow, but not steep enough to waste lumber and heat in the winter. A dirt floor, we decided, would not only be the simplest, but also the least expensive and best for the Museum's boatbuilding and repair needs. Experience has shown that a damp dirt floor helps to prevent the drying out of hull planking. It also reduces dust and cushions carpenter tools if they happen to fall, and it allows for digging under a boat when certain keel repairs are called for. Alternatively, wooden floors would, we felt, be best for the lean-tos.

Our next step was to determine how high the lean-tos ought to be to allow for a good joiner shop, with a rigging loft above it, on the west side; and a stockroom, office space, heating plant, and space for a big ship saw and planer on the east side, with a visitor viewing balcony above. We wanted good windows for light and air in both the main shed and the lean-tos, which would be simple to wall off and separately heat come winter.

Good ventilation is of prime importance in any wooden or metal shed. The structures themselves need it. Boats, tools, supplies, and lumber need it. And, of course, human beings need it–lots of it. Ventilation is not difficult to arrange in the type of shed we contemplated. Hot air rises, and opening windows or vents high up in both ends of the main structure would assure a good circulation of air, as needed. It is no doubt carrying imagination a bit too far to compare our proposed shipyard shed to a Gothic cathedral. But there are similarities in both design and use. The lean-tos do act as buttresses to add strength and stability to the whole structure without creating a clumsy, bulky appearance. The central work space–or nave, if you wish–does glow with a natural light from above. As for the work performed in a boat shed. . . .

Holy or otherwise, the plan of the Ships Committee did gain the approval of the trustees. Following the spring construction of a lumber storage shed to demonstrate the viability of our plan, building of the main shop began in the fall of 1970. These and the other shops and sheds that followed were sited more or less parallel to the flow of the river and the Museum waterfront at its southern end. The roof-peak lines thus ran roughly north and south, establishing a neat, practical, and harmonious cluster.

Our own shipyard personnel, under the direction of Maynard and Gene, did the actual construction work. By doing it ourselves–a procedure later dubbed "the

With the lumber shed complete, the Shipyard main shop takes shape in February 1971. Photograph by Lester Olin . (Mystic Seaport 1971-2-105)

Mystic way"–the Museum not only saved a lot of money compared to contract work, but helped form and train a good shipyard crew and created an inventory of machinery and equipment that the shipyard would need in its primary mission. When the facility itself was up and running, that work on the boats and ships would begin in earnest.

A long one-story paint shop went up somewhat to the east of the main shop and parallel to it, giving us a protected outside work area. An existing building (the one built over the railway in which to restore the Noank smack *Emma C. Berry*) was floated downriver and landed at the south end of the yard; it later served as our machine shop. During this period, we were fortunate to have Calvin Bogue as one of our yard crew. Calvin was a jack of all trade, a blacksmith, a fine mechanic, a man of wit and imagination. He understood what the shipyard's needs would be and helped meet those needs economically as well.

The biggest and most important item of shipyard equipment that we had to plan out and build was the lift dock. Although there were several engineers among us, none of them felt adequately qualified to design this specialized unit,

The lift dock is a girder framework decked with wood and suspended between two finger piers with concrete piles. Electric motors in the two low buildings reel and unreel cables that pass through a series of sheaves to move the platform. The dock was designed with a lift capacity of 375 tons—enough to hoist any of the Museum's vessels out of the water. In this early test in September 1973, a construction barge is lifted. Photograph by Mary Anne Stets. (Mystic Seaport 1973-9-164)

which involved a combination of dredging, pile-driving, a big elevator platform that would raise and lower by means of cables, sheaves, winch drums, chain, and sprocket drive systems–and a big electric motor.

We knew about the Blount shipyard's lift dock in nearby Warren, Rhode Island, and knew that it had operated successfully and was of about the same size and capacity as that we were looking for. Mr. Blount kindly gave Maynard the name of the Hingham-based engineer who had designed that lift dock, and thus we became acquainted with Al Bates of J.E. Bowker and Associates. For many weeks Al drew plans and made frequent visits to Mystic. He was almost wholly responsible for the entire design of our lift dock.

In building the dock we assumed the role of general contractor ourselves. With Al's help we split the job into several separate tasks, then hired subcontractors to create what Al's drawings called for. By working on the lift dock with Al and the contractors, we minimized costs and gained a complete understanding of how to operate and maintain this complex and absolutely essential piece of equipment. Our 375-ton capacity lift dock has proven to be an excellent hauling and launching unit. Although costly to maintain, it has put Mystic Seaport in a unique position of being able to handle ships' maintenance and repair entirely on its own.

Knowing what work the shipyard would be faced with, Maynard and his crew were in an excellent position to plan and anticipate. I don't remember many instances, if any, where things had to be done over. From my point of view, the Museum had by 1973 created a splendid foundation for a permanent shipyard that could be expanded and improved in efficiency as time went on.

6
Tall Trees and Ship Timber

I have said that a carefully planned lumber storage shed was the first building to be built at the Museum shipyard. The reason for this is easy to explain. Suitable lumber must be on hand and safely stored before one can reasonably undertake a proper boat maintenance or rebuilding program.

Yet since World War II it has become increasingly difficult to locate or obtain many of the wood species that have over the years proven to be most suitable for the different components of a vessel's construction. I lack the space or the knowledge to do more than touch on a few of the most obvious illustrations of this situation–and to suggest why it is no longer possible merely to call in an order to a good lumber yard and expect to get what is needed quickly, if at all.

Specialized boat lumber must first be located, then acquired, and, finally, specially processed before it is ready for use. Consider, for example, hard pine, a wood traditionally favored for ship's planking and one of the reasons for the long life of the *Charles W. Morgan*. The best hard pine is known as longleaf yellow pine. It is clear, straight-grained, fairly heavy, and very strong. Its heartwood, being full of pitch it does not readily absorb water and is therefore very resistant to rot. As I know it, this pine grows in the South, especially in Georgia, and takes as long as 200 years to mature to its best quality. The great virgin stands of this wonderful wood were largely consumed years ago in the construction of naval and commercial vessels and, later, mill buildings and the like. Other types of yellow pine were and are available, but little remains of the quality that the Museum needs for its work.

In the early 1930s Percy Chubb II called me one March evening to ask if I would like to join him for a small house party he was planning at his father's plan-

A splendid specimen of eastern white pine. Photograph by Lucy Bixby. (Author's collection)

tation in Thomasville, Georgia. This is a part of the world renowned for carefully managed sport shooting of quail, dove, and wild turkey. Although I am not a master of the shotgun, I do like young ladies and outdoor sports, so I accepted at once.

In addition to giving us a grand two weeks of shooting at Springwood Plantation, the house party produced other results. Most importantly, Percy Chubb fell in love with his guest Corinne Alsop and subsequently married her. I myself fell pretty hard for another guest, Barbara Childs, but only a lovely friendship followed, not wedding bells. I date my wonderful lifelong association with Percy and Corinne Chubb from that Springwood shooting party. I also credit Springwood with having given me a deep admiration for and a faith in the majestic longleaf yellow pine trees that were so conspicuous at Thomasville.

When we came to look for hard pine at the Museum's shipyard, I immediately thought of Percy and discussed with him (and then with other members of his family) the possibility of procuring some of the Springwood trees. Through the Chubbs, we received an introduction to a most knowledgeable and cooperative second generation Thomasville forester, Leon Neel. Leon oversaw the care of the Springwood trees, as well as the care of trees on other plantations in the area. In due course, Maynard Bray went down to see Leon. He came back with an arrangement whereby Leon would set aside for the Museum good virgin hard pine trees that were destined to be cut out for one reason or another. When he had collected a flatcar of these logs, he would ship them, full-length, north to us. We would off load them in New London or a siding in Mystic and truck them to the Museum for processing, storage, and eventual use.

A stand of longleaf yellow pines. (Courtesy Tall Timbers Research, Inc.)

Among other information I later gathered from Leon is that the best virgin hard pines grow on virgin soil. Soil that has been used for other agricultural products is in some way chemically altered, so that the hard pine that grow on it is different from–if not actually inferior to–virgin growth timber.

Mystic Seaport paid for these precious logs in various ways, depending on the circumstances. (Leon Neel himself was generally paid by the plantation owners.) A few landowners were pleased to have their trees used to prolong the life of a worthy Mystic vessel and let us have them as a gift. Others had cooperated with us as to price. All our suppliers have shown an active interest in the work of the Museum.

A massive live oak, with its long and sinuous branches.

Another species of hardwood that was of utmost importance in the construction of the *Morgan* and other sawn-frame vessels of the past is live oak–so called because its leaves keep renewing themselves and its foliage remains alive and green throughout the year. Live oaks also flourish in the south and especially so in Georgia and South Carolina. They are large and long-lived trees. The angel oak is estimated to be some 900 years old. These trees grow with a big short trunk and many long outreaching branches that are formed with sinuous curves and angles. The wood, although hard, strong, and durable, is obviously not useful for houses or other shoreside construction, but it is ideal for the sawn frames and other structural members of vessels that have so many different shapes in their hulls.

Locusts on the shore of Lake George, New York. Photograph by Lucy Bixby. (Author's collection)

Live oak is understandably difficult to come by. However, Mother Nature interceded on the Museum's behalf in the form of Hurricane Hugo's march through Georgia, in 1989. The shipyard staff learned about this massive blow-down, and Quentin Snediker made arrangements with local storm-clearing authorities to cut the fallen trees into lengths suitable for ship work. These heavy pieces were then trucked up to the shipyard for future use. This transaction was a bargain in the best sense of the term, in that the deal was equally beneficial to both buyer and seller.

Perhaps the locally grown hardwood the Museum uses most for ship repair and building is what I call native white oak. It is a great wood for keels, steam bent frames, deck beams, and other framing components. Mystic Seaport's marine architect, engineer, draftsman, wood expert, and all-round wonderful gentleman, Bob Allyn, who came to the Museum in 1969, led us to an excellent source of white oak that was located on nearby property owned by a water company. They were clearing out a stand of oaks and were glad to help us acquire a fine supply of excellent oak logs and get them from the stump to the shipyard for safe storage under cover. Here was another true bargain for all concerned.

Locust is a second hardwood available locally. It has been used in boatbuilding for centuries. Being an attractive color as well as hard, strong, and exceptionally durable, it is great for ship rail stanchions, rails, cleats, tillers, trunnels, and the like. In fact, it is one of my favorite woods, to the extent that all Concordia yawls are trimmed on deck and below in locust. Although locust grows in southern Connecticut and in many places around the world, it is not usually available in lumberyards. However, we found several sawmill operators who were willing to collect as many locust trees for us as we needed. They did not know what to charge for them. When I suggested they treat them like native oak, they said, "Why not?"

Native eastern white pine used to be plentiful, and it grows beautifully in New England. It is a soft but durable wood. Before World War II it was a favorite house-and-furniture building material. One of the Concordia 31-foot sloops is now 60 years old, and her white pine planking is still in excellent condition. In 1939, when Katy and I built our house in Padanaram, we paid three cents a board foot for excellent quality white pine. Although it is still available, it now costs a dollar or more per board foot when purchased in lumberyards.

In storage after being sided in the Museum's sawmill, these hackmatack knees show the root-trunk angle that makes ships knees such essential structural supports in traditional wooden shipbuilding. Photograph by Nancy d'Estang. (Mystic Seaport 1996-11-64)

Only a few years ago Mystic Seaport negotiated through a contractor for the Nature Conservacy to acquire several loads of the famous cathedral white pines located in Cornwall, Connecticut. Many of these trees were in excellent condition, despite having been blown down by a tornado or twister. This purchase was a third bargain: the fine, long logs were ideal for deck planking, spars, and other special Museum projects.

In Maine and Nova Scotia grows a tree from which excellent boatbuilding knees can be made. This is the hackmatack or larch–one of the needle species, not of the leaf family, but not evergreen either, for its needles turn brown in winter. Like other trees that grow in damp ground, its roots tend to extend outward in a shallow pattern and not down with a deep taproot. In spite of this root system, the hackmatack does have at least one major root that often grows out from the trunk at a right angle, developing a structure in which the grain follows the angle and, when freed from the other roots, makes a perfect knee.

Because of their specialized and outmoded use, hackmatack knees are no longer to be found in lumberyards or in the secondhand market. After a serious search, however, the shipyard staff did find a man in Cherryfield, Maine, who made a business of identifying likely hackmatacks and cutting them to preserve one good knee. It seems wasteful to sacrifice a whole tree for one element, until you consider that the knee will become an essential member of a unique vessel. Furthermore, our commission gave the woodsman one more winter cutting hackmatack trees–and hackmatacks continue to grow in abundance.

As the shipyard takes shape in December 1970, Gene Baudro demonstrates the sawmill to trustees, including the author (nearest the camera). Photograph by Russell A. Fowler. (Mystic Seaport 1970-12-60G)

There are of course many other species of wood that are used in boatbuilding and shipbuilding, among them fir, spruce, cedar, etc. However, I fear that in my enthusiasm for wood I may have overworked the subject already. So now let me write a little about what must be done to a log before it becomes useable wood.

Once procured, boatbuilding logs must be custom milled to fit the specifications for the particular job at hand. Much of the milling procedure I've already touched on in writing about the construction of *Integrity*. However, I should mention here that while the shipyard was being set up, Mystic Seaport purchased a good secondhand sawmill and installed it just north of the main shop and adjacent to the lumber storage area. The mill was useful in occasionally getting out some of the conventional stock for the new sheds, but it became absolutely essential for the milling of ship's timbers. In no practical way could the milling have been carried out by an outside contractor.

At the same time, the shipyard acquired a good jointer and two big planers. Each was essential for general carpentry as well as for boatbuilding. A fourth piece of mill machinery bought secondhand was a tilting-head bandsaw, known as a shipsaw, that could be used for general purposes, but had been specially designed for shipbuilding. It allows a heavy piece of timber to roll through, lying flat on the saw table, while the band saw blade tilts to achieve different bevels.

A fifth vital piece of machinery was a big sparmaking lathe nearly 90 feet in length. This arrived in 1974 from Owens Yacht Corporation. Although this was not of immediate use in constructing the shipyard, it has allowed the shipyard to turn masts and spars for its own vessels as well as a big flagpole for the town of Mystic, a and foretopmast

Under the watchful eyes of Maurice Baron and Jeff Pearson, the saw makes its way through a live oak log. Photograph by Mary Anne Stets. (Mystic Seaport 1991-7-131A)

To operate the shipsaw, or tilting-head bandsaw, one man pushes the timber through while the other adjusts the bevel by wheeling the head along an arc that changes the angle of the bandsaw blade. Photograph by Nancy d'Estang. (Mystic Seaport 1993-8-264)

for the tall ship *Gazella Primeiro*, and wooden shafts for the Saugus Ironworks restoration in Massachusetts. Quietly but surely, the Museum was working its way into a unique position to exhibit, maintain, and restore or rebuild as needed a live fleet of traditional boats and ships.

As I wrote in my introduction to Benjamin Mendlowitz's 1994 *Calendar of Wooden Boats* (Brooklin, Maine: NOAH Publications, 1994), wood is essential to the welfare of our world. Trees are living wonders in themselves. The wood that comes from trees has continuing life of its own whenever man wishes to make use of it to improve his well-being. Be it lofty cathedral or country church, stately mansion or humble cottage, king's throne or my favorite pine chair, wood has forever been used to enhance the quality of life. Most stringed instruments and many woodwinds use a combination of several varieties of wood to produce the instrument's unique tone. Great concert halls achieve their fine acoustics with wood. Thomas Edison, having invented the phonograph, never found the tone he sought until he discarded his metal loudspeaker horns for wooden ones.

For many of us, wood remains the material of choice for the building of our boats. In some ways, a wooden boat is much like an orchestra, in that every detail of design and construction must play its part to create the perfect whole. Wood offers the boatbuilder so many wonderful basic luxuries that do not simultaneously exist in other materials. It unobtrusively mutes unwanted noise, yet enhances sounds that we like to remember. It is a friendly insulator against too much heat or cold. It lessens troublesome vibrations and is kind to the touch. With its various soft colors pleasant smells, and different textures and grain patterns, wood not only serves its main purpose, but also decorates and adds charm and beauty.

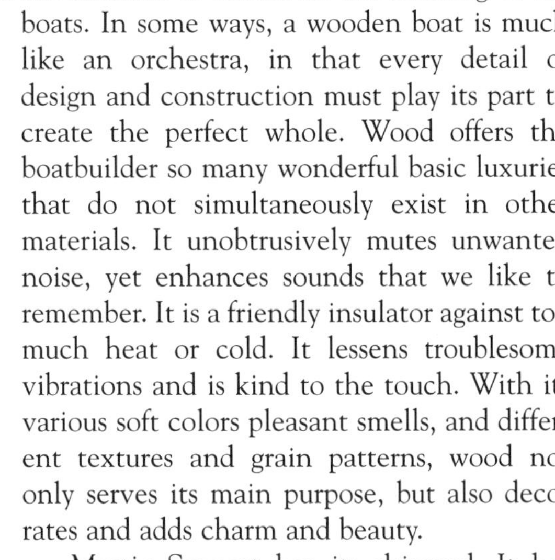

Mystic Seaport has its shipyard. It has suitable machinery to operate the shipyard. It

Cal Bogue adjusts the cutting head of the spar lathe as it moves back and forth along a track beside the spinning timber that will become the *Charles W. Morgan's* new mizzenmast. Photograph by Ken Mahler. (Mystic Seaport 1974-3-212)

has suitable timber with which to repair, build, or rebuild vessels in the shipyard. Now I, with others, dream of a museum woodlot in southeastern Connecticut–and perhaps even one in Georgia–as an enduring future source of boatbuilding lumber. The Museum has taken an important step in this direction by planting some eastern white pine and spruce trees on one of its nearby properties. May the woodlot expand into a forest. May a new age of wood begin.

Under restoration from the keel up, with her white oak frames and yellow pine planking, the sardine carrier *Regina M.*, one of the Museum's earliest watercraft acquisitions, shows off her graceful form in the shipyard shop in 1993. Photograph by Nancy d'Estang. (Mystic Seaport 1993-5-74)

CLOSED

7
Refloating the *Charles W. Morgan*

Soon after the trustees approved the building of a shipyard at Mystic Seaport in the spring of 1970, all thoughts turned toward the idea of refloating the *Charles W. Morgan* so that she could be towed to the shipyard, hauled out on the liftdock, restored as necessary, and then put on exhibit as she should be, afloat in her native element.

The idea was not without its critics. At an early meeting, a few of the trustees asked whether it wouldn't make sense to leave the *Morgan* in her sand bed and just make a cement underbody for her, like a cellar beneath a house. She would thus look as she did and at the same time her underwater maintenance would be eliminated. Others pointed out the advantages of using aluminum spars and synthetic sails and running rigging on the vessel. After all, most yachts were heading in that direction for reasons of efficiency and economy.

This line of thinking puzzled most of us, because we thought the objective of Mystic Seaport was to preserve and commemorate the accomplishments and activities of days gone by. On the other hand, it does take all kinds to make the world go around. More important still, it takes many kinds of minds and attitudes–both forward- and backward-looking–working together to keep a museum alive and vibrant.

Perhaps two anecdotes will help explain my own position. The first concerns Suzie, an active member in the mid-1970s of the Mystic Seaport "Mod Squad," officially the Special Demonstrations Squad. The Squad was a group of young folks whose mission was (and still is) to demonstrate various historic activities along the Museum waterfront, including such routines as climbing the rigging of the *Morgan* and, in the usual quiet air of the morning, setting some of her sails,

Recaulked and repainted above the sand berth she occupied for 32 years, the *Charles W. Morgan* is nearly ready for refloating in November 1973. Photograph by Lester Olin. (Mystic Seaport 1973-11-44)

then taking them in and furling them late in the afternoon; rowing and sailing whaleboats; and acting out other traditional shipboard and longshore tasks.

Suzie, along with several graduate students in the Museum's summer Munson Institute, was living in one of the Mystic Seaport-owned houses across the street from the Museum's main office. At the time, I was doing some extended research on my first book at the Museum's G.W. Blunt White Library (a most wonderful and enjoyable source of maritime information, I must add), and I too was temporarily quartered in the same house across the street. Suzie was not only a delightful and very capable young woman; she also made delicious whole-wheat muffins. These we would eat as we had breakfast together in the kitchen, all the while swapping yarns of mutual interest.

One morning Suzie told me about a busman's holiday the Mod Squad had taken to Newport, Rhode Island, to see a replica of HMS *Rose*, a British frigate that was there on exhibit. The first thing the squad noticed was that the ship's squaresails were hanging from their yards in disarray. They learned from a sailor on duty that the ship's crew was, frankly, unable to furl the sails properly. The Mod Squad immediately offered to go aloft and do the job right. It was then that Suzie and her friends learned that the sails were made not of traditional cotton canvas, but of some slippery new synthetic fabric that made it difficult, even dan-

A summer demonstration of whaleboat rowing on the Mystic River off Lighthouse Point, 1974. The Museum's Special Demonstrations Squad was formed in 1972 to perform maritime skills aloft, on the water, and on the ground. Their demonstrations around the Museum's waterfront have been a very popular way to help visitors understand how a square-rigger works, how a whaleship like the *Morgan* hunted whales, and how the U.S. Life-Saving Service rescued shipwrecked crews. Photograph by Claire White-Peterson. (Mystic Seaport 1974-6-127)

gerous to furl in the traditional manner. The Mystic crew was eventually able to do an adequate furl. In doing so they learned that it was a grievous mistake to dress a traditional square-rigger in new-fashioned synthetic sails.

Neither Suzie nor I dared to think what complications might develop if the *Morgan* were to be rerigged with aluminum yards and Dacron running rigging. Might the spars act like paper men in a gale of wind? And what sort of friend would a slippery synthetic line be to a struggling seaman 70 feet in the air? Given the racket one Dacron halyard can make on a small sloop's aluminum mast, neither Suzie nor I could bear to imagine the rata-tat-tat a square-rigger could make if fitted out with combinations of aluminum and Dacron from stem to stern, from truck to deck. From this I came to the firm conclusion that, for reasons of amenity, safety, historical integrity, and economy, Mystic Seaport's exhibits must always be as authentic as we can make them.

A second anecdote involves a fellow trustee whom (because he is a composite of several individuals) I will call Jim. Jim was a friend and a man of importance. He served on a number of Museum committees. He was one of the Museum's most loyal and supportive members. The fact that Jim's thoughts about the Museum sometimes sailed on a different tack from mine prompted me to ask him if he had the time and inclination to take a walk through the Seaport with me. He was happy to oblige.

Our first stop was the Shipyard. Here I showed Jim our fine and unique supply of ship timber, the traditional and active rigging loft, several recent repair jobs, and the like. I also talked to him about the plans and aims of the Ships Committee to carry out work as authentically as possible. Jim was courteous and patient and let me chatter on. But the only time he seemed really excited was when he noticed several yard workers experimenting with featherweight, rubber-powered model airplanes during their lunch break. Obviously knowledegable about aeronautics, he stopped to try a few experimental flights of his own. Since my own understanding of aeronautics is just about nil, I was content to watch.

On our way back for lunch we passed by *Glory Anna II*, a little ketch-rigged, double-ended Block Island "cowhorn." Her natural cotton sails were partially raised and lazily drying in the light midday breeze. I couldn't help stopping to express my admiration for this exhibit. Jim was silent for a moment and then said with a friendly smile, "Yes, it *is* charming, Waldo. But I do have to believe that you are one of those fellows who is content to follow along in the paths of your father and grandfather." Clearly Jim's eyes were looking at a primitive old boat that would benefit from some latterday improvements. My eyes saw a beautiful little ship that had been just about perfect for the Block Island fisherman who sailed the likes of her in days gone by.

By now I concluded that my morning's efforts had been mostly in vain. Jim might be a friend, but he would never share my vision of Mystic Seaport. It was only much later that I slowly came to learn the real lesson of the morning we had spent together. For while Jim may have lacked my particular passion for the past, he did not lack passion for Mystic Seaport and what it represented. Living largely in the present and dreaming richly of the future, Jim was able to support and lead the Museum we both loved in ways that I could never approach.

So much for parables.

While the shipyard was being built, all of us were thinking about the challenge of refloating the *Morgan*. A primary trustee concern was whether the old ship would safely float if we put her back into the water. She had, after all, been sitting in a bed of sand for some five decades, and we had no way to inspect the exact condition of her bottom and keel. As a first step, Curator Ed Lynch hired two outside professionals to help him with the technical issues that were involved. His first recruit was naval architect Bob Allyn.

Embedded in sand and still wearing the paint scheme with false gunports first used on the ship when she went on display at Round Hill in 1925, the *Charles W. Morgan* is rigged for Christmas 1970. Photograph by Lester Olin. (Mystic Seaport 1970-12-174)

Because no lines plan was available, Bob's first order of business was to make up a reliable set of plans that would allow him to make displacement and stability calculations. The ship's old stone ballast had been removed. Now, before refloating, it was essential to determine just how much new ballast to install and where to place it. Too little and the ship might be top-heavy and capsize; too much and the ship might float too low to negotiate our local water depths of about 12 feet. With the ship's bottom hidden in the sand, Bob had a very difficult assignment. With cooperation from other shipyard staff, however, he did a first-class job producing the plans and numbers we needed. Then and there he became a permanent and indispensable member of the team.

The other professional Ed Lynch hired as a consultant was Dr. Merrill of Penn State University who was well known and respected as a wood technologist. He took hundreds of borings–core samples–from the *Morgan*'s hull, some short, some long, and had them analyzed in his laboratory for type, condition, percentage of rot, etc. He then worked these facts and figures into a comprehensive scholarly treatise that was of some present value to Bob Allyn and that will remain a fascinating document for maritime historians. His study did not, however, come to any positive conclusions as to whether the *Morgan* in her current condition would float safely. In the end, that decision was left to the Ships Committee.

The Museum's naval architect, Bob Allyn, at his transit during preparations for the refloating of *Charles W. Morgan*, October 1973. After a long career as a naval architect at the Electric Boat shipyard designing elements of the most modern of watercraft, Bob joined the crew of the Mystic Seaport Shipyard to document the most traditional of American watercraft. Photograph by Mary Anne Stets. (Mystic Seaport 1973-10-97A)

From our own observations, members of the Ships Committee believed that the *Morgan* would float satisfactorily and without resorting to a canvas shroud wrapped around her hull or other aids. But, as always, I discussed matters with Henry Jarvis, a fine old shipbuilder who had come to the Museum in 1968 as the *Morgan*'s lead shipwright. I caught up with Henry one noontime. He was eating his lunch up forward in *Morgan*'s fo'c'sle. It was a cozy spot, then partially roped off from visitor traffic, heated by a wood stove, and lighted by a ship's lantern. I came right to the point. "This ship will float if we launch her, won't she?" I asked. Without a moment's hesitation, Henry said, "Of course she will. She's been floating right along on every high moon tide."

You may wonder why it was so important to refloat the *Morgan*. There were, in fact, many reasons. Once afloat she could be towed to the shipyard and hauled out periodically for routine maintenance or extensive repairs. She would roll with the pats and punches of even light breezes. Rain water wouldn't settle or puddle in low spots, but would instead automatically spill out and dry off. Likewise, dust and dirt would be less likely to lodge in corners and crevices. In strong winds the ship could heel well over and greatly lessen sudden, heavy strains on rigging, spars, and the hull itself. Afloat, the ship could be shifted in position at will so that concentrations of sun and wind would not always be striking the same area. And from a visitor's point of view, even a slight motion aboard the ship would make her a living exhibit and add a critical extra dimension of reality to her being. Sails set on spars that move gently against the sky catch and please the eye far more than those that are stiff and static.

The decision to refloat the *Morgan* was made in August 1970. Now the question became: "How do we accomplish this?" Here again the trustees discussed things at length without arriving at a clear plan. Meanwhile, the Shipyard staff

Downrigged and partially excavated, the *Charles W. Morgan* waits for a tide to float her free, November 1973. Photograph by Lester D. Olin. (Mystic Seaport 1973-11-43)

was making good progress with a plan of their own. They decided to put the question to Bill Molloy, a New London-based marine contractor with whom the Shipyard had worked before and whose equipment was just what was needed. But as things turned out Molloy's other dredging commitments forced him to engage Bob Holbrook of Westbrook, Connecticut, as a subcontractor to do the digging.

The first I knew about all this was when I saw an ancient steam dredge alongside the *Morgan*. With puff-puffs of white steam, she was digging an ever-bigger hole ahead of herself and creating an ever-growing "island" along the side of the river channel. It was obvious that the work made an intensely popular exhibit for Museum staffers and visitors alike. Already the newly created island sported a handsome sign reading "Anderson Island," in honor of the shipyard's master rigger.

The whole plan was simple and practical. In no way did it disturb other Museum activities. The idea was to dig a big enough hole in the right place so that the *Morgan* could be encouraged to slide sideways into it. I wasn't there when conditions first seemed right to push the old ship into the hole. However, I am told many hands pushed and a tow boat pulled . . . with no result. Several more tries still proved unsuccessful. Further efforts had to be postponed until the morning of December 6, when high tide was again due at 5:00 A.M.

But I was there before dawn that morning. Having been advised of the new refloating schedule, I jumped out of my bed in Padanaram, fired up my faithful 1941 Plymouth, and headed for Mystic Seaport at flank speed. As I was parking at the Museum, I could see in the gathering light that *Morgan* was still in her prison of sand. Then, before I could reach her, even at a full run, I saw her give a little shudder . . . and slip calmly into the hole at ten minutes before five. I thought to myself, "Good old *Morgan*, she waited for me," and joined the crowd of cheering onlookers. Henry Jarvis's prediction had been accurate. Floating, the *Charles W. Morgan* leaked scarcely a drop.

After having underwater profile measurements taken of her keel so the lift dock could be blocked to match it, the *Morgan* was towed to the Shipyard and hauled on the newly completed lift dock. And so the refloating of the *Morgan* had come to glorious completion–a tribute to the Henry B. duPont family and the shipyard that they had endowed.

With the *Morgan* afloat at her new berth behind him, Director Waldo Johnston addresses the crowd assembled for the rededication of the ship in June 1974. This was the culmination of five years of hard work and a proud moment for Mystic Seaport. Photograph by Mary Anne Stets. (Mystic Seaport 1974-7-383)

8
A New Wharf for an Old Ship

With the *Charles W. Morgan* now having proven she could float and on her own bottom, we could proceed to create a permanent berth for the ship and build it while she was being worked on at the Shipyard. Certainly she should be on display in the water and shown to her best advantage in the approximate location of her former sand bed. She should lay to a stone wharf, since that is what whaleships did when they were at home in New Bedford. Only in this way would she be as secure as possible and look her part and do her job of forming an authentic, tangible link between present and past.

To have the opportunity to create an appropriate wharf at this time was a wonderful thing. It was also a very serious challenge. In pondering the matter of the *Morgan*'s berth, I found it strange that, generally speaking, very little seemed to be known or recorded about wharves, docks, piers, and the like. Even the terms themselves were somewhat hazy, at least in my mind. The boatyard structure I had bought in Padanaram Harbor from Colonel Green's estate had always been known as South Wharf. Originally it had consisted of a stone *pier* built out by the harbor channel and connected to the shore only by oak piles and wooden decking. Later this wooden connection was replaced by two stone walls with earth fill in between.

Just south of South Wharf is what Padanaram locals have always called the yacht club *dock*. This consists of a wooden walkway on oak piles, with finger *piers* extending out on each side. Years ago, when it was commonplace to go to Europe by ocean liner, we used to board the ship at a named or numbered *pier*, where the ship was *docked*.

Under nearly full sail, the *Morgan* lies at her berth on the south side of Chubb's Wharf in 1993. Photograph by Claire White-Peterson. (Mystic Seaport 1993-4-93)

In an effort to clarify at least some of the nomenclature, I searched through an old encyclopedia, only to find that *wharf* was not even indexed. *Pier* was a name given to a solid support of masonry or brick which carried an arch or other similar structure—or the *mole* or *jetty* used to shelter a harbor. *Pier* also applied to a structure built out into the water with piles, for use as a landing place. *Dock* was a term commonly used as synonymous with *wharf* or *pier* for the loading or discharging of vessels, cargoes, or passengers, and in a more restricted sense applied to floating or stationary structures for the building or repair of ships. *Dock* was also, and perhaps more properly, the slip or waterway extending between two *piers* for the reception of ships. From this developed the verb to *dock* a vessel.

Regardless of the original or etymologically accurate meanings of these terms, the structures that were used by whaleships in New Bedford were known as *wharves*. So, *wharf* it had to be for the *Charles W. Morgan*.

In a romantic sense, wharves have a charm for almost everyone. We have gone "down to the wharf" to see our ship off or to await her arrival. We instinctively know of the importance of wharves and the fact that they form a main link between land and sea. Why, then, have they received so little attention in written or pictorial records while ships have received so much? I suppose that ships are more striking and impressive in their motion and their beauty. Like the foundations of our houses, and perhaps of our lives, we tend to take wharves for granted.

All over the world, harbors have been an important factor in the development of the surrounding countryside. It is not always the best harbors, however, that have become the most important shipping centers, but more generally the ports with the best inland access as well as the best wharves and docking facilities. Consider a few well-known seaports. Newport, Rhode Island, for example, is one of the great natural harbors, but has not been a big shipping port since the 18th century. New York has both a big natural harbor and the facilities to accommodate a huge fleet. Baltimore would not seem to have a great natural harbor, but has made itself into a major shipping center. I guess the point I am trying to make is that Mystic Seaport's waterfront, as well as her ships, must continue to receive thoughtful attention if its image as a whole is to have true meaning.

All this set me to wondering just why New Bedford should have become a great whaling port. It did indeed have a good deepwater harbor, well located for small New England sailing ships. And obviously it had developed suitable wharves from which to conduct the whaling industry. So it seemed that learning about the old wharves of New Bedford would be of real importance in planning for the new *Morgan* wharf. As a starter I revisited the New Bedford waterfront. There I found, as I had expected, that many of the old whaling wharves were, in whole or in part, modified or otherwise, still in existence. Many were still in use. To me this is a great tribute to those who planned and built them 150 or more years ago. How did they do it? That was the next question.

A New Bedford wharf, ca 1885. It is stone-faced and earth-filled, with wooden caplogs. A downrigged whaling bark lies alongside. At the next wharf the bark *Niger* dries her sails. William H. Tripp Collection. (Mystic Seaport 1973.899.153)

The New Bedford wharves are all basically built of rough stone, with two or three faces carefully fitted and placed to form an even, strong outer surface. The upper areas, especially the caps, are often hand-split and of a more rectangular shape. The stone itself is always granite acquired locally. Wooden extensions and fender piles are obviously later additions, and surfaces of the wharf fill must have changed from time to time to suit the current need. This is about all I could see with my own eyes. So being unable to find any detailed literature on the subject, or any living 150-year-olds to interview, I had to piece together my conclusions from a few general articles, some photographs of the period, and a few firsthand experiences of my own.

Clearly it must have been desirable to locate a wharf near deep water and where the land approach would be practical for traffic on wheels. Protection in bad weather had to have been a consideration. And in those days of sailing ships without power, the direction and force of tidal currents would have been another consideration. Prevailing winds would also have made a difference in planning the angles and location of a wharf. The length and depth of vessels to be berthed would have dictated the size of the wharf. Likewise, the cargo to be unloaded and perhaps temporarily stored would also have dictated its area. Routine maintenance of the vessels as well as extensive overhauls had to be accomplished at the wharves, which were always busy places and centers of activity.

John F. Leavitt's sketch of the proposed Chubb's Wharf, with the *Morgan* on the south side. (Mystic Seaport 1974.61)

Needless to say, while I was making my own investigations Museum staffers were busy on the same project. Don Robinson worked most productively with the Army Corps of Engineers and other governmental agencies to get the necessary permits. John Leavitt made a splendid sketch of the proposed wharf with the *Morgan* alongside to give the trustees and staff a good visual idea of the project. Bob Allyn, in consultation with Maynard Bray and others in the Shipyard, was working out a cross-sectional plan for the walls of the wharf, its perimeters, and other elements.

Maynard was the one who did the general planning for the final size and shape of the new wharf. Its length was to be such that the *Morgan* could lay to either side and face either the shore or the channel. Its width was to be sufficient to allow her to lie across the end. Thus, she could be berthed to take advantage of prevailing summer winds to set her sails–or to gain protection from winter gales. In case of a hurricane, she could heel a bit and move slightly with the gusts. This arrangement would always leave two berths open for visiting ships.

The main office staff was, of course, anxiously projecting the cost of the wharf. To employ a big marine contractor would be very costly, involving high labor expenses, distance from contractors' headquarters, special equipment, and elaborate construction drawings. It seemed to some trustees that a new permanent wharf for the *Morgan* might be months, even years away.

For these reasons alone, it seemed that the plans of the Ships Committee for doing the job "the Mystic way"–by the Museum itself–would be worth a serious look. I raised the subject with Trustee Percy Chubb, who immediately took a personal interest in the idea. He agreed that a stone wharf would be essential for exhibiting the *Morgan* to her best advantage. Granite in the form of ledges along the coast, in the mountains, or wherever it exists, had played a big part in holding New England together. To cut granite into usable pieces and assemble them properly in buildings, wharves, breakwaters, or other structures is never easy or cheap. Once accomplished, however, the results can be lovely to look at, relatively easy to maintain, and rewardingly permanent. Percy was more than enthu-

Corinne and Percy Chubb aboard *Antilles* at Peter Island, 1972. I am standing by the mizzen. The Chubb family has long been a major force in the field of marine insurance. Thomas Caldecott Chubb was born in London, England, at about the same time that the *Morgan* was being built at New Bedford, in New England. He and his son Percy (I) were founders of Chubb & Son of New York. Hendon Chubb, often called "the dean of American insurance," was Percy's younger brother and a man of outstanding ability and charm. It is in memory of this great man that the surviving members of the family donated a wharf for the *Morgan*. Hendon's wife, his son and daughter-in-law, Percy (II)'s, Corinne and their six children, and the wife and children of Percy (II)'s late brother, Thomas C., all joined together to make this a family memorial. Unidentified photographer. (Author's collection)

siastic. He soon informed the Museum that he and his family wished to create a worthy memorial to his father, Hendon Chubb. Work on Chubb's Wharf began in the early spring of 1974.

The final drawings indicated that Chubb's Wharf was not to be exactly rectangular, but rather shaped so that the end would run parallel with the channel. In overall dimensions the wharf was to be approximately 150 feet long and 100 feet wide. As there is only about two and a half feet of tidal rise and fall in the Museum basin, the height of the walls was figured at only seven feet above mean low water and thus would be the same height as the other Museum wharves and bulkheads. Any higher and access for visitors (or cargo) would be difficult.

After calculating the approximate size of the stones needed for the wharf walls, Maynard and I hoped that nearby Stonington, Connecticut, or Westerly, Rhode Island, might be a good source of supply. We explored several old quarries in both towns and found many stones that might be useful to us. In the end, however, we had to face the fact that the quarries were no longer active and that there was no practical way we could get those heavy stones to the Museum.

At this point Bob Gillette, a Museum member and Concordia yawl owner, entered the picture. Bob had close connections with the Rock of Ages Company in Barre, Vermont, the famous monument makers. Bob discussed our situation with their management, who were most cooperative. They had good granite on hand that they were not using, and they could economically get it out and ship it down by rail to New London for us. Maynard made a trip to Barre to discuss our particular requirements. Soon, big suitable stones began coming our way. Thus yet another member of Mystic Seaport had stepped forward to solve a serious problem for us.

In New London, Maynard made arrangements to rent an available railroad siding for temporary storage of the stones–and also a crane to handle them. Here the stones could conveniently be picked over and sorted. The system worked out perfectly. The big supply of stones, ranging in size up to six or more tons, took almost no Museum space and caused no serious confusion on the Museum grounds. A hired truck picked them up as needed each day and delivered them direct to the crane that would set them in their allotted place in the wharf walls.

For the actual construction work, Bob Holbrook helped us again with his equipment and wharf-building knowledge. Working from the shore outward, he made sure that small stones and gravel fill kept pace with the progress of the wall. No waterborne crane was necessary. As for the choice and placing of each stone,

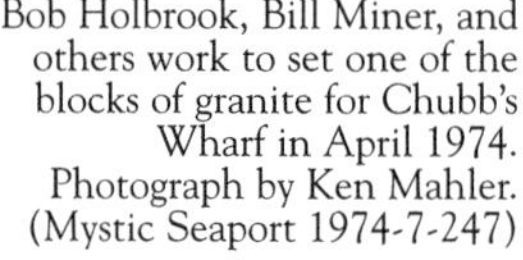

Bob Holbrook, Bill Miner, and others work to set one of the blocks of granite for Chubb's Wharf in April 1974. Photograph by Ken Mahler. (Mystic Seaport 1974-7-247)

major credit goes to a retired wall-builder, Bill Miner, working with a long pole to establish footings beneath the water and to guide the crane operator in placing stones precisely where they belonged.

The construction of Chubb's Wharf worked out well. Overall costs were less by far than professional estimates. By working to our own plan, we ended up with a wharf that looks its part and serves its purposes well. Far from being a distraction to the Museum staff or visitors, wharf construction proved to be a fascinating exhibit, constantly evolving and changing. During the construction, the Shipyard staff became more familiar with stone construction and maintenance, and with the equipment needed for such work–all good omens for the future. Finally, we had some control of the timing and had the wharf ready for the *Morgan* right after initial repairs to her bottom had been completed, and only about six months from when she refloated and temporarily abandoned that very site. She returned to the completed Chubb's Wharf in June amid great fanfare.

On August 9, 1974, during the Museum's annual meeting, Chubb's Wharf was formally dedicated by Percy Chubb II in memory of his father, Hendon. The *Charles W. Morgan*, with her rig back in place, stood proud alongside. Once again a worthwhile project, accomplished "the Mystic way," became a permanent and integral part of the Museum.

With the *Morgan* in the background, Percy Chubb conveys the wharf to William C. Ridgway Jr., president of the Museum's Board of Trustees. Photograph by Mary Anne Stets. (Mystic Seaport 1974-9-63)

Hauled out for the first time in nearly 60 years, the *Charles W. Morgan* rests on the shipyard lift dock a month after being refloated. Photograph by Thomas Lamb. (Mystic Seaport 1974-1-41)

9
Rebuilding the *Charles W. Morgan*

By the summer of 1974 it was generally agreed that the *Charles W. Morgan* should be completely overhauled and that now was the time to start the process. After all, she had been through 80 years of strenuous whaling–from 1841 to 1921–in many different parts of the world and under various owners and masters. Then, for another 70 years she led a busy and confusing life in the New Bedford area, first as a motion picture prop, later as an exhibit ship at Colonel Green's Round Hill estate, where she suffered through the 1938 hurricane. At Mystic Seaport, starting in 1942, she had for more than 30 years been on display in a bed of sand and without adequate maintenance. No question about it, the *Morgan* was overdue for some serious attention. Fortunately, Mystic Seaport was now ready to give her the attention she needed.

Having had a direct, if minor, part in the designing and construction of *Integrity*, I viewed the basic process of building a sawn-frame vessel as straightforward. One started with the backbone and keel, with rising stem at the forward end and rising sternpost at the aft end. On this structure one set up the crosswise frames or ribs. To this skeleton one fastened watertight planking on the outside and heavy sheathing called ceiling on the inside. Then one added the deck beams and decking on top all strengthened by bracing knees and other elements. The *Morgan* was in essence simply a bigger *Integrity*.

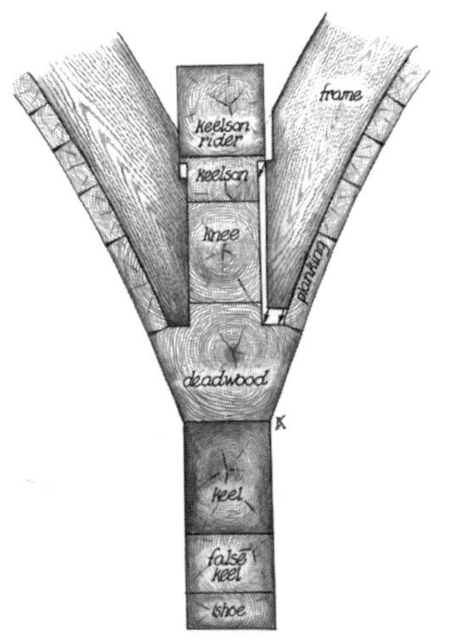

A cross section of the *Morgan*'s backbone. Drawn by Kathy Bray. (Mystic Seaport 1983-3-51)

To build a new *Morgan* would have been a comparatively easy undertaking; however, this approach was understandably never given serious consideration. The *Morgan* had become a National Historic Landmark in 1967. To retain this honor, she herself had to be preserved and authentically restored as the oldest wooden whaleship in the world. Furthermore, the restoration, the taking apart, and the piece-by-piece renewing would reveal historic construction details and in many cases help to uncover hidden stories from her long career. Mystic Seaport's Trustees officially confirmed the decision to restore.

The next and logical question for both trustees and top management to ask was, of course, how much all this was going to cost. The question was in the end one for the Ships Committee to try and answer; but, really, it was an impossible puzzle to solve with precise and finite numbers. Restoring would be a very long and difficult process. There was just no way of telling exactly how long it might take or what unexpected problems would reveal themselves as work progressed. We had to solve the riddle of costs in a different way.

Our suggestion was that work on the ship continue year-by-year in open-ended fashion until the task was complete. First we would figure our labor costs for a year–so many men at such and such wages–then add overhead on our equipment, and then include a reasonable estimate for materials. To help with this last factor, we noted the experience of many shipyards where cost of materials have tended to run at about 30 percent of labor costs. Following this method, we could figure with some accuracy what our annual budget would be, assuming that our entire shipyard labor force would consist of approximately 35 men. With this budget in hand we could proceed to restore the *Morgan* and the rest of our fleet as rapidly as practicable, keeping in mind the need for authenticity, the order of Museum priorities, and the important fact that fine shipwork in progress would be one of our very best exhibits. We knew we could not expect always to remain exactly within budget, but this method of controlling costs has so far [1995] proven helpful and realistic.

Realizing what an important part labor played in our estimates, it may seem arbitrary to have settled on a specific number of men for the shipyard. But after you have figured out carefully what you are going to be doing, you do seem to come up with a particular number to make the best team: not too many; not too few. Our projection went something like this:

1 yard director	1 electrician
1 office secretary	1 stockroom clerk
7 shipwrights	3 mechanics
4 painters	1 naval architect
3 riggers	1 keeper of records
4 maintenance workers	2 yardmen and 3 shipkeepers

It was important that most of these people be versatile in their skills and be willing to help out on any reasonable project. Teamwork is just as essential in a shipyard like ours as it is on a football field. It makes for efficiency and good morale, and at Mystic Seaport both of these virtues have been very much in evidence. Changes in yard personnel have been very gradual over the years. Also in our favor is the fact that interesting jobs requiring good skills, important responsibilities, and the use of pleasing materials can be and usually are rewarding. Although various excellent crew members have left for one or another reason, after a time, some of these have returned. A number of the older men who have retired have since returned to work on a part-time basis or on special projects. As in most successful enterprises, the Shipyard crew is a vital Museum asset in which we have a big investment. We cannot afford to lose good workers if we intend to have and to hold a museum that lives up to its reputation as one of the best in the world.

Developing a plan and a yard crew were not the only challenges the Museum faced in the *Morgan* restoration. As previously mentioned, for example, no measured drawings existed for the ship. The shape of the vessel had undoubtedly been developed from a half-hull model approved by her original owners. Probably the construction methods and lumber specifications were determined by the experience of the builder. For our project we needed complete plans (drawings) to work from. Bob Allyn had to develop these plans from information gathered wherever he could find it. For a rough lines plan he had to rely on measurements taken from the ship herself. This had been very difficult while the bottom was buried in the sand. It became easier after the ship was hauled.

Making up construction plans for the ship as she had been when first built was far more complicated. During the *Morgan*'s 130 years of hard work and varying duties, many repairs and alterations had been performed on her. These changes often made it difficult for us to determine what work was original and what was of more recent date. Thus, restoring the *Morgan* in a completely authentic manner was, to put it mildly, an ambitious goal, one that few other museums would be in a position to undertake now or ever. Building replicas of vessels, yes. But not restoring an historic ship for scholarly and educational purposes, as well as for exhibit. The difference is very real. And while our project was not as difficult as returning a scrambled egg to its original condition within the shell, there were some similarities, as you will see.

Using an adze, Roger Hambidge shapes a live oak timber for the *Morgan*.
Photograph by Nancy d'Estang. (Mystic Seaport 1996-11-34)

Despite the complications, the Museum did have many unique advantages that worked in our favor. The Shipyard and lift dock were now fully operational.

Don Robinson (left) and shipwrights load spars from Washington state onto a float for the upriver trip to the Shipyard in 1977. Photograph by Kenneth E. Mahler. (Mystic Seaport 1977-5-191)

Chubb's Wharf was completed and at the *Morgan*'s service. The yard crew was growing in size and experience, and it had already begun extensive retopping work on the *L.A. Dunton* and continuing restoration on the *Joseph Conrad.* Maynard Bray was a very competent shipyard manager and had, among other able employees, two experienced old-time shipbuilders to consult with: Basil Tuplin and Henry Jarvis. A younger shipwright, Roger Hambidge, had recently joined the crew and was to have a vital part in future renovation work. Charlie Anderson was a fine old-time rigger of wide experience, having spent many years as rigger at the Electric Boat shipyard in nearby Groton, Connecticut, as well as time under sail at sea and he was a fine mentor to promising younger riggers.

And other factors, too, were helpful in furthering the goal of historical accuracy in our work. We had extensive research material in the Museum's G.W. Blunt White Library and in our vast photographic archives. We had been given complete access to the photo collections of the New Bedford Whaling Museum and the Kendall Whaling Museum. And ultimately we had a special shipyard associate, Nancy d'Estang, to collect record, and consolidate information relating to the *Morgan* and her construction from every imaginable source. Nancy's accomplishments will continue to benefit the Museum and maritime scholarship in general long into the future.

Henry Jarvis and Charlie Anderson

Henry Jarvis (left) and Charlie Anderson, two men who contributed immeasurably to the refloating of the *Morgan* and her welfare at Mystic Seaport. Henry Jarvis had a long career in boatyards and on a yacht skipper before coming to the Museum. Charlie Anderson rounded Cape Horn in a grain ship as a young man. Later, as head rigger at the Eelctric Boat shiyard, he supervised the crews that hoisted and swung the nuclear reactors and other sophisticated equipment into their tight spaces in nuclear submarines. After mos t men are retired he was still working back in sail as Mystic Seaport's head rigger. What fascinating yarns Henry and Charlie spun while spinning oakum on board. Photograph by Mary Anne Stets. (Mystic Seaport 1977-11-11)

Let me now review the rebuilding process for the *Morgan* in a brief and general way. Work on the vessel started in 1973, and it took the shipyard some 20 years faithfully to complete the task. Rebuilding the hull took the first ten years; the second ten years were taken up reassembling and renewing as necessary the interior of the hull and the deck structures. By 1993, the ship's condition was such that she could be considered almost entirely authentic.

The Shipyard took pains to cooperate with other Museum departments in keeping its three major ships in the water and on exhibit during the summer months as much as possible. The Ships Committee and my smaller subcommittee were always closely involved in the work. But the Shipyard and its crew made most of the decisions and did all the hard work. When Maynard Bray resigned as a full-time staff member to move to Maine in 1975, Jim Giblin and then Don Robinson took over Maynard's duties. More recently, Dana Hewson and finally Quentin Snediker have directed the shipyard. I became an emeritus trustee and naval architect and boatbuilder Joel White became chairman of the Ships Committee. However, Joel allowed me to remain on the Committee, and there were no significant changes in the Committee's direction or continuity of effort.

The work continued on the *Morgan* without interruption. For the first seven years, she was often hauled out and sometimes left on the lift dock in the winter. She lay at Chubb's Wharf almost every summer. From 1981 through 1983 she had to remain continuously out of the water for major work. But during those years she had a plastic cover framed over her, allowing work to continue and visitors to view operations and go onboard from strategically placed wooden walkways. This was the period when the hull of the ship was substantially retopped with new frames and new planking on the outside. One by one, each old main deck beam was replaced with a new one, and then a new deck was laid. All specifications faithfully followed those used by her original builder. By the fall of 1983, she was in a

Housed over on the lift dock for all-seasons work, the *Morgan* receives her new stem apron. Photography Mary Anne Stets. (Mystic Seaport 1983-1-90)

Inthe *Morgan*'s hold, George Emery (left) and Jeff Pearson lever the new stem apron into place. Photograph by Mary Anne Stets. (Mystic Seaport 1983-1-912)

This drawing shows the complicated structure at the *Morgan*'s stern, where the rudder head passes through the rudder box behind the sternpost and is mortoised for the tiller. Drawn by Kathy Bray. (Mystic Seaport 1982-8-5)

This drawing shows the *Morgan*'s deck framing, including the frame (rib) heads and extended bulwark stanchions (right), the deck beams and their anchoring lodging (horizontal) knees, and the intermediate deck beams. Drawn by Kathy Bray. (Mystic Seaport 1982-5-94)

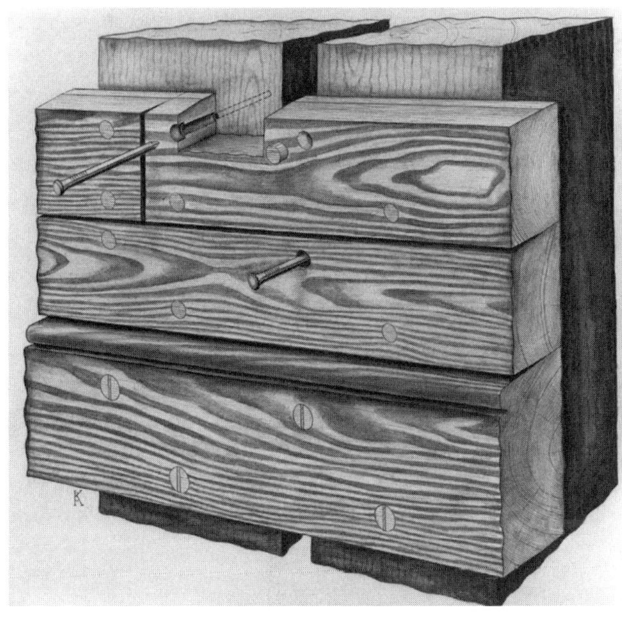

In this planking diagram, the thicker wale strake with beaded edge is fastened to the frames with wedged locust trunnels. The planks are fastened with copper spikes, covered with bungs. Note the caulking seam created by beveling the plank edges. Drawn by Kathy Bray. (Mystic Seaport 1982-5-40)

This drawing of the *Morgan's* hold shows a deck beam with hanging knees, the step for the foremast (lower foreground), several stanchions, the two strengthening riders installed in the 1880s to reinforce the bow for Arctic whaling, and the stem apron. Drawn by Kathy Bray. (Mystic Seaport 1985-3-105)

The sailor's view, looking in from the *Morgan*'s bowsprit. Photograph by Gary Adair. (Mystic Seaport 1986-6-288)

condition to go back into the water. In May of the following year she was ceremoniously rededicated.

The following few winters several big, final construction jobs were planned out and accomplished, the most challenging of which were new stem and sternpost assemblies. It had been impossible to do this until the shape of the vessel was held in place by the retopping. The huge timbers involved in the stem and sternpost work were painstakingly constructed on shore and then fitted into the hull. After that the Shipyard replaced or renewed the 'tween-decks and the deck structures.

One day Maynard Bray phoned to tell me that the *Morgan* needed a new and longer mizzenmast for rigging her, once again, as a bark and that the Shipyard's search for a suitable replacement had come up empty. Did I by any chance have a suitable mast up my sleeve?

I did! We met in Padanaram and drove out together to the Round Hill Beach, formerly owned by Colonel Green but now belonging to the town of Dartmouth. Not far from the location of the *Morgan*'s long-vanished Round Hill berth stood one of Colonel Green's tall radio poles. It was near perfect in height and diameter. The town of Dartmouth said that we could have it. The next day the same riggers who had launched the schooner *Integrity* for me came, cut down, and delivered to Mystic Seaport the *Morgan*'s new mizzenmast. The Museum's Shipyard completed the job.

The *Rachel B. Jackson*

In 1984 I introduced my young friend George Emery to the Museum. He and his brother, Jim, had with their own hands just finished completing a fine little schooner that they honored with the name of their grandmother, *Rachael B. Jackson*. Although their plan had been to use the schooner in the charter business, Jim had taken a job ashore and George had joined the Mystic Seaport Shipyard crew for a spell. He lived aboard the schooner and worked as a lead shipwright. From the very first, he proved a great asset to Mystic Seaport.

For a few days before, during, and after each of the 1984 and 1985 trustee meetings, Katy and I chartered the *Rachael B. Jackson* to live aboard and to serve as a meeting place for our subcommittee and for anyone else who had a particular interest in the progress of the *Morgan*'s rebuilding and other shipyard activities. I cannot claim that these meetings were as momentous as the conferences held in Japanese waters on the battleship *Missouri*, but we did cover a lot of ground both in regard to the *Morgan* in particular and to Mystic Seaport in general.

Revell Carr, Mystic Seaport's director (and later also its president) and, Frank Kneedler, the associate executive vice president, usually stopped by with a greeting, a question, or a bit of late news. Percy Chubb often came aboard (with his familiar greeting, "How are things, good, bad, or indifferent?"). Board chairman Cliff Mallory was always welcome and always had some enlightening input. One one occasion, that great deepwater yachtsman Drayton Cochran spent the night aboard and joined in our deliberations and spoke with enthusiasm about the boatbuilding course he was taking with John Gardner—in sessions held just a few yards away from where the *Rachael B. Jackson* was berthed. And so it went, and I always felt well-primed for the formal shoreside meetings of the trustees and the Ships Committee.

In 1986, George Emery and the *Rachael B. Jackson* sailed away from Mystic Seaport for other adventures. However, our subcommittee continued to meet–on other ships as available. Really, there is no better place for such gatherings than the deck or cabin of a well-found vessel in a lovely harbor like Mystic's. Quiet early morning breakfasts, noontime sandwiches, and twilight or evening sessions encourage serious thinking and enhance understanding. I only wish more trustees, staff members, and friends of Mystic Seaport could regularly meet under the same circumstances and absorb the enduring virtues and attractions of this unique seaport museum.

The schooner *Rachel B. Jackson* underway with a party on board. (Mystic Seaport 1983-3-1)

JULY 1990

10
Building the Bulkheads

So far I have only written about the rebuilding of the *Charles W. Morgan*, but of course there were many other vessels at the Museum that took their turns at the duPont Preservation Shipyard, either on the lift dock or inside the main shop for routine maintenance or minor repairs–or for extensive overhaul or restoration. This ongoing work is of real interest to the visitors, who can watch it from the gallery inside the main shop. The entire fleet was gradually being brought into good condition and kept that way.

But Mystic Seaport's ships and boats are only part of the story. From the beginnings of the Museum's development, and in some cases before, most retaining walls and docks had been built of wood: oak pilings, fir or hard pine decking, and so on. The dock where visitors viewed and boarded the *Morgan*, for example, had originally been built in 1942. The creation of wooden bulkheads began in 1947. Lighthouse Point, being near the channel, was one of the first areas to get attention. Then came the basin north of the *Morgan*. In 1952 the South Dock area was bulkheaded. The landfill south of this is where the Shipyard now stands.

As I have said earlier, the stone Chubb's Wharf was built in 1973, and a few years later it was obvious that many of the wooden bulkheads were showing their age and would soon need serious attention. To rebuild these structures in kind would doubtless have been the quickest and cheapest solution. There were, however, other salient factors that the trustees and administration had to consider at this point. We all knew that stone bulkheads would be more costly, but would also, once completed, be far more durable and less expensive to maintain. But to many of us, there was an even more cogent reason to favor stone. Historically, after all, whaling ports like New Bedford had used granite as the practical mate-

In light of his inspiration and encouragement, the Museum's bulkheads were dedicated to the author in September 1990. Photograph by Mary Anne Stets. (Mystic Seaport 1990-9-105)

rial for their waterfronts, and the objective of the Museum was to create, insofar as possible, the components of a genuine historic seaport.

In due course the decision was made to explore the ways and means of renewing the waterfront using granite walls. Don Robinson, who was then in charge of the Shipyard, spearheaded the investigation and contacted a number of marine contractors. Several were interested in the project, but not unexpectedly, estimates ran high–ranging generally between four and five million dollars. Unless there was a miracle, these costs would put the stone bulkheads permanently into limbo.

Nevertheless, we all kept thinking and hoping. And the thinking of the subcomittee was that, given its success in the building of Chubb's Wharf, Mystic Seaport should be able to create the stone bulkheads itself. In the end, that thinking prevailed. Some funds were donated that enabled the Shipyard to plan and start building the stone bulkheads in 1980 "the Mystic way."

Don Robinson was in charge of the whole operation. First Don worked with Bob Allyn to develop formal engineering plans for the areas concerned. These plans had to be drawn both to facilitate construction and to be in a form acceptable to the various government agencies having oversight of such work and granting approval for it. Don did a wonderful job negotiating with the Soil Conservation Service. He knew clearly what Mystic Seaport wanted to do and how it would be doing it. The soil conservation officers, in turn, understood the plan and were in a position to provide the cost of materials we needed for the job. The only restrictions placed on our work by the Department of Environmental Protection and the Army Corps of Engineers were understandable–the main one being that, to protect aquatic life, we only do underwater work during the winter months. With this initial negotiation completed, the Army Corps of Engineers also approved our plans.

Even before the paperwork was completed, Don Robinson was looking for a new source of suitable granite. The Rock of Ages Company (which had furnished the Chubb's Wharf stones) was by this time in new hands, and rail shipment of stone from Vermont had become too expensive. However, Don did locate stone from abandoned quarries in Westerly and from certain stone structures that were being demolished. These stones could be transported by truck to the bulkhead site.

As for equipment needed, Don acquired most of it secondhand: a 35-ton crane with which to set the heavy granite blocks; a second big forklift to unload the blocks (some weighing five or six tons) and move them around as needed; and a compressor to cut and drill and drive sheet pile for the base. This left a major piece of equipment that we had to have: a barge on which to mount the crane and from which to work. After a careful search, Don found in Jersey City, New Jersey, a used steel barge of the right size and for the right price.

Block by block, the granite bulkhead at the south entrance nears completion in 1982. Photograph by Mary Anne Stets. (Mystic Seaport 1982-7-5)

The barge was good, but how we were going to get it to Mystic? Here again, thanks to our Shipyard facilities, "the Mystic way" worked to our advantage. Just a few months earlier in 1979, the Electric Boat division of General Dynamics had presented the Museum with a welded steel tugboat that had become too small for their submarine program. The tug was already in good working order for a trip to and from Jersey City. Captained by Don, an experienced sailor and ship-handler, and manned by three seagoing members of the Shipyard crew, Mystic Seaport's newly acquired towboat *Kingston II* steamed down to Jersey City, hooked up to our steel barge, and towed her safely back home and up the Mystic River to the Shipyard. It was a fine and wholly professional piece of work.

Meanwhile, our versatile mechanic Cal Bogue was putting the newly acquired crane in good working order for use on the bulkheads. While it was still mobile on land, he drove it over to the south parking lot and practiced operating it by picking up heavy granite blocks and placing them in new positions. As soon as the barge was available, he worked with Don Robinson to lay out her deck arrangements, which included a spud system for holding the barge in position and equipment such as an air compressor and the crane for jetting and pile driving, as well as the crane for lifting and setting the granite blocks.

With the barge so outfitted and in operation, and a basic crew of three good men backed up by additional Shipyard personnel as needed, the Shipyard commenced work on the bulkheads in the fall of 1980 and continued through the

As he had during the refloating of the *Morgan*, Cal Bogue spent hours underwater during the bulkheading project, directing the positioning of the granite blocks and chinking the spaces between them. Photograph by Mary Anne Stets. (Mystic Seaport 1983-1-146)

next five years, when they substantially completed the work. As with the building of Chubb's Wharf, the project did not disrupt the Museum's daily programs. On the contrary, it provided an interesting show for the off-season visitors: jetting, pile-driving, or setting granite blocks in place. Something new every day. As for me, I just watched the process when I could and complimented the crew on their accomplishments.

Cal Bogue is the one who deserves top honors for building the bulkheads. His work was spectacular. He not only handled the jetting, drove in the sheet pilings that supported the above-water granite, and picked out the stone blocks, but, donning his diving gear, he also went underwater and directed the setting of each block. In the underwater work, which included chinking the walls as needed, Cal had help from a volunteer, Fred Wilson, who set up a system for telephone contact between diver and crane operator. The Shipyard had other volunteer help, as well, and the whole project was a prime example of teamwork and adaptability "the Mystic way."

I don't know if anyone ever tried to figure out just what the bulkhead building costs came to. I do know that some of the labor costs had already been accounted for as part of the normal operation of the Shipyard. As to materials, including steel pilings, granite blocks, grout, and fill, the Soil Conservation Service covered this big item. The new equipment was, of course, an added expense. Even considering its episodic use, however, it was certainly less expensive to acquire and operate our own equipment than to lease it from an outside contractor. Besides, the equipment could be sold or be on hand for future Museum needs–along with a crew expert in its use. "The Mystic way" saved the Museum several million dollars at least.

For those of us committed to "the Mystic way," there was one more important piece of business to accomplish. For surely it was time for the Museum staff and trustees to beef up the department for maintaining Mystic Seaport's buildings and grounds similar to the organization of the Shipyard. Such an entity would help keep Museum costs within annual budgets and make the institution less reliant on outside contractors.

Although grounds and building maintenance may seem less glamorous than the work of a shipyard, it is surely of equal importance to the overall health and welfare of the Museum. Revell Carr, Frank Kneedler, and other senior administrators agreed that every Museum department would gain from having a champion and cheerleader, preferably a trustee knowledgeable in that area and keen about it, who had time to work on it and promote its needs and sell its virtues to the board of trustees.

In due course, Mystic Seaport organized an official Buildings and Grounds Committee with James L. Giblin, a newly elected trustee, as its first chairman. I had gotten to know Jim well during the years he was an important member of the Museum staff as director of the Operations Department and after that while he briefly ran the Shipyard. He is a great sailor and has owned some fine traditional boats. The Museum was very sorry to lose him when he took a job elsewhere. But we were all delighted to have him back, this time as a board member and as head of an important new committee.

With enthusiastic leadership and an enlarged crew, the now renamed Facilities Department of buildings and grounds was in a position to make its own contribution to "the Mystic way."

7

11
Yachting History and Mystic Seaport

From its first days, Mystic Seaport–then formally known as the Marine Historical Association–had an interest in yachting and sought to trace the roots of American pleasure-boat design. As early as 1931, the Museum acquired *Annie*, a 29-foot racing sandbagger sloop built in 1880, and put her on exhibit. Other small pleasure boats were added each year, including several designed and built before World War I by Nathanael G. Herreshoff that are, in my opinion, examples of the very finest boat shapes ever created.

The first of the Herreshoff 12 1/2-foot sloops appeared in 1914. These little boats were designed by Herreshoff for use in and around Buzzards Bay, where winds and waves can often be boisterous. Almost immediately they became popular for both daysailing and racing. They were smart, able sailers, easy to handle and safe for all ages. Years later I chartered an enlarged version of the Herreshoff 12 1/2- footer that was known as a Herreshoff 16-footer (21 feet overall) or the Fish Class. In fact, Katy and I used one of these for our honeymoon cruise. As I write this, the Herreshoff 12 1/2-footers are still going strong as a class in New England waters, and several of the Fish Class sloops are still actively sailing individually.

Herreshoff 12 1/2-footer under sail on Buzzards Bay in 1951. Quite similar to New England and Bahamian workboats in form, this was by far the most popular Herreshoff design. About 360 of these boats were built in wood, and almost 900 of the design were built in fiberglass as the Bullseye. The watercraft collection at Mystic Seaport includes *Nettle*, one of the first group of 12 1/2s built by Herreshoff in 1914. N.G. Herreshoff changed the scale of this design to produce the five-foot-longer Fish Class sloop in 1916. About 40 Fish boats were built between 1916 and 1936, and many are still in sailing condition. *Merry Hell*, one of the last built, is in the collection at Mystic Seaport. Photograph by Norman Fortier, neg. 4728. (Courtesy of the photographer)

Another lovely Herreshoff creation is the 26' sloop *Alerion*–a cabin daysailer N.G. Herreshoff had built for his own use in the winter of 1912-13. Herreshoff used this model as the basis for his Newport 29 class sloop. Although the first batch of Newport 29s came out in 1914, three of them have remained active and have raced competitively and successfully in recent years. Captain Nat's son Sidney modified the Newport 29, when in 1926 he designed the Fishers Island 31-foot class of sloops–the boats that later got me into the boat business. After

Bahamian fishing sloops *Blue Wing* and *Spray Hound*, Georgetown, Great Exuma, 1985. The resemblance between these splendid working sloops and the Herreshoff 12-1/2 and 16-footers is remarkable and unmistakable, even to the sail plans that feature large gaff mainsails and small jibs. On close inspection, however, it is clear that these workboats have a deeper forefoot than the Herreshoff pleasure boats and are not as delicately molded. Photograph by the author. (Author's collection)

that, Captain Nat's son L. Francis kept this model in mind as he designed Paul Hammond's 72-foot ketch *Landfall*, on which I raced to Plymouth, England, in 1931.

In 1985 I visited Georgetown, Great Exuma. Blanche Borden Frenning, whose father had once owned the Herreshoff schooner *Ingomar* and whose great-grandfather, General Benjamin F. Butler, had for so many years owned the yacht *America*, had invited me to stay at her lovely place on Goat Cay. She, Linton "Bunny" Rigg, and Colonel Art Herrington had all been involved in organizing the annual Out Island Regatta, and because of these connections I was to have a front-row seat in Blanche's launch to follow the racing fleet. Bahamian sloops came from far and near, and I had the opportunity of a lifetime to observe and take pictures of these lovely traditional sloops.

Walking across the dock at Goat Cay soon after, a sight struck my eye like a bolt of lightning. There, resting comfortably on their sides and stern-to, appeared to be two Herreshoff 12 1/2-footers. I went to have a closer look. Only then did I discover that they were not products of Bristol, Rhode Island, but fishing boats modeled and built at Great Exuma. In spite of being slightly larger than the Herreshoff 12 1/2-footers and much more heavily built, their shape was delightfully similar. The bow underwater was slightly deeper, but the midship section and the transom looked to me almost identical.

Naturally, I took many photographs and made inquiries about the history of these native craft. From Jack, a Bahamian who worked for Blanche Frenning, I

At the Museum's Small Craft Weekend in 1971, the author sails *Solitaire*, a handsome Kingston lobster boat built by Edward Ransom about 1885. Her hollow garboards and counter stern were inspired by *America*'s Cup defenders of the period, and she was built for pleasure use, not for lobstering in Massachusetts Bay. Rebuilt by Concordia Company for Michael Sturges, head of the Museum's education department, she stepped lively, even with a gaff mainsail smaller than her original sprit-rigged main. The annual Small Craft Weekend, begun in 1970, offers many boating enthusiasts the opportunity to share and try such classic small craft. Photograph by Russell A. Fowler. (Mystic Seaport 1989-4-22)

learned that his father had been a boatbuilder and that the boats I admired were based on models that went back well into the 19th century. Here, then, was a hull shape that had persisted in Bahamian workboats for 100 years and more–and that had, as skillfully modified for pleasure-boat use by N.G. Herreshoff in 1914, been a popular model in American waters for another nine decades. So far.

It gave me a thrill to know that a good shape for a boat remains a good shape indefinitely. This may not be quite as simple as the principle that a circle makes a good wheel, but it is not far different. And I firmly believe that the range of small craft that Mystic Seaport has been collecting has much to tell us about human creativity in many fields other than boating.

In 1976 Mystic Seaport organized the first annual Antique and Classic Boat Rendezvous. It has since become a great attraction for the Museum and, with its parade down the river, for the Mystic area as well. Being an antique myself, I have been invited to be one of the Rendezvous judges each year. This has been a great pleasure for me in that many of the participating boats are old friends that I have enjoyed observing and sailing during my years on the water.

Another acquisition that has greatly enhanced Mystic Seaport's holdings is the world famous Rosenfeld Collection of yachting photographs. As early as 1930 and continuing for many years, I seldom attended any important yachting event, be it the start of an ocean race, a New York Yacht Club cruise or regatta, or an

Morris Rosenfeld's distinctive and ubiquitous F.K. Lord-designed powerboat *Foto III*, without which no important race start seemed complete. Launched at City Island, New York, in 1929, the 33' *Foto* (their third boat of that name) served the Rosenfelds through the 1960s. Here she is off Newport, ca. 1960, with Morris at left and Stanley at right. Alongside is the 45-foot George Crouch-designed cutter *Nicor*, which was launched at City Island in 1937. Photograph by Norman Fortier, neg. 8624. (Courtesy of the photographer)

America's Cup race, without becoming aware of Morris Rosenfeld and his sons and their beautiful little 33-foot chase boat, *Foto*. She was everywhere, and with her was Morris or one of his sons clicking away and, always, in the right position for the perfect photograph.

When I was working on the first volume of this autobiography, I was anxious to get good photographs of three boats in particular, and I arranged to meet with Morris's son Stanley one morning at his downtown New York office. I was on time. In fact, I was a little early. His office building was far smaller than I had expected, but inside the entryway a small sign assured me that I was in the right place, and I ventured into a tiny lift that let me out into a minute (and very dark) hall. I knocked on the only visible door. No answer. I peeked through the mail slot and saw only darkness. Then I took the elevator back down to the tiny lobby and returned to the sunlit street. Here I found a bench, sat down, and tried to plan my next move.

When I saw a lean, energetic man with a big flat package under his arm, I felt sure my visit would not be in vain. And so at last I met Stanley Rosenfeld and gained entrance to his office–a plain, long room with windows at the street end and walls lined with open shelves and endless rows of cardboard boxes.

Ingomar during her racing days. In the glorious era of the great racing schooner yachts *Ingomar* stood out as one of the greatest. She was a steel vessel, 127 feet overall (87 on the waterline) designed and built by N.G. Herreshoff in 1903 for Morton Plant, a prominent yachtsman of wide experience. She had a successful first season in New England waters. Then in 1904, under the command of the immortal professional racing skipper Charlie Barr, she sailed to Europe, where she proved her winning ways in England and in Germany, outsailing the Kaiser's new *Meteor* in convincing fashion. During World War I *Ingomar* changed hands several times, eventually losing part of her keel to the war effort. In 1922 she was snatched from the ship breakers by Mrs. Spencer Borden, who had the sporting courage and determination to complete the purchase on very favorable terms. The Bordens sold *Ingomar* in 1929, after which the schooner fell on hard times. She was lost off Cape Fear on February 24, 1931, the very day that Mrs. Borden herself died. Photograph by James Burton. (© Mystic Seaport, Rosenfeld Collection B1984.187.121).

"Well, what can I do for you?" Stanley asked with a friendly smile. I asked if I could order a print of *Ingomar*, a 127-foot Herreshoff schooner built in 1903; of *Flying Cloud III*, a 67-foot Hand schooner built in 1924 for Lawrence Grinnell; and lastly, of *Lexia*, a 64-foot gaff-rigged English cutter built in 1932.

Stanley seemed slightly puzzled by the selection. "Why these particular boats?" he asked. When I told him that I had been to sea in each of them, he seemed pleased. "I think I can help," he said. And so he did.

A good print of the *Ingomar* he quickly located on one of the long tables set up in the center of the office. He had evidently made it not long before for another customer. There was no sign of me among *Ingomar*'s afterguard, and for a good reason: the picture had been taken in 1904, before Stanley or I was born. Negatives of *Flying Cloud III* and *Lexia* he easily found, too, and in both of these I was much in evidence: at the helm in the first, as part of the crew lined up on deck in the second.

How could I not have been impressed by the beauty, volume, and breadth of

At the Museum's 1988 rendezvous of Concordia yawls, the author talks with J. Revell Carr, then director and president of Mystic Seaport. Revell came to the Museum in 1969 and was named curator in 1970. In this role he was actively involved in the efforts to refloat the *Morgan*, to refine the Museum's exhibits, and to elevate the publishing program, among many other accomplishments. He replaced Waldo Johnston as director in 1978 and served until 2001. His hard work, vision, and inspired leadership characterized and defined "the Mystic way." Photograph by Mary Anne Stets. (Mystic Seaport 1988-9-180)

the Rosenfeld Collection–or delighted when, in 1984, Mystic Seaport acquired this unique and historic archive of historic yachting and maritime images? It is the best collection of its kind in the world, and it is now safely preserved and accessible at Mystic Seaport.

In 1985, Revell Carr established at Mystic Seaport a Yachting Committee under the leadership of a great competitive sailor, Timothea Larr, and with other Trustees and serious sailors as members. This committee has been very active and has served to significantly expand the Museum's already vast yachting-related collections and bring them to national and international attention. A year after the Yachting Committee first met, the members endorsed an oral history program in which a skilled professional, Fred Calabretta, searched out older key figures in the sport and in the supporting endeavors such as yacht building and designing. He captured their memories on tape. Two years later, Timmy Larr and her committee inaugurated a two-day Yachting History Symposium that has further strengthened the Museum's commitment to yachting in the most inclusive sense. The first winner of the newly established William P. Stephens Award for exceptional contributions to the sport and the art of yachting was designer Olin J. Stephens II.

Little by little Mystic Seaport has expanded its yachting horizons. It has sought, received, cataloged, and safely stored for future use and study yacht plans from an ever-growing range of American and British yacht designers. It has accessioned many forms of yachting memorabilia, including yacht club yearbooks, boatbuilders' sales brochures, and marine catalogs, and it has become home for the archives of the Cruising Club of America, the Seawanhaka Corinthian Yacht Club, the Star Class, and other boating organizations.

12 Always Back to Boats

Conditions, particular and general, change for most of us as the years go by. Nonetheless, my guiding star seemed always to lead me back to boats, whatever my age or circumstances. First it was sailing boats for the joy of it. Then it was taking care of boats as my vocation. Finally, along with my interest in the work of Mystic Seaport, I had wonderful opportunities to keep sailing for the joy of it, mostly with Katy and old friends.

During the summers, surrounded by our children and grandchildren, Katy and I were at our place in Padanaram. I continued to cruise and race, especially on friends' Concordia yawls. One summer Katy and I joined Percy and Corinne Chubb for a European cruise aboard their motorsailer *Bird of Passage*. Starting in Ireland we sailed north up the Irish Sea to Scotland and then through the Caladonian Canal and across the North Sea to Norway. There we were guests at a Norwegian salmon fishing club that could trace the ownership of its salmon pool back to the 14th century, and there I became acquainted with traditional salmon fishing prams that were almost identical to the Bateka model of pram that we provided as tenders for Concordia yawls.

During retirement winters we lived on Captiva Island, which is one of the barrier islands off the west coast of Florida. We had acquired a lovely piece of bayside waterfront property from Padanaram friends, Mr. and Mrs. Allan Weeks, who had searched the world over for a semitropical home where they could do a little farming and a lot of gentle boating. Here we built a boathouse long enough to shelter the 19-foot Pete Culler-designed-and-built sailing skiff *Dixie Belle*, and wide enough to include a few gardening and carpentry tools, as well as boat gear and–importantly–a desk at which I could work on my writing. The setup was per-

Dixie Belle, the 19' sailing skiff that Katie and I used during our winter visits to Captiva Island, on Florida's Gulf coast. I asked Pete Culler to build me a slightly enlarged Good Little Skiff, and he completed her in 1970. She was absolutely perfect for our boating plans and pleasures under oar or sail. With her shiny oil-darkened rails, her tapered green sheerstrake, her soft yellow topsides and red copper boot top, she was a lovely sight for most any eye. To some, her heritage was identified by the star at her bow and the crescent moon at her stern. With her sprit rig and tanbarked cotton sail, she was uniquely herself and blended in so beautifully with the natural charms of her Captiva surroundings. She is now in the watercraft collection at Mystic Seaport. Unidentified photographer. (Author's collection)

Bikie Brooks's 65-foot *Uncle Jack* was built in Florida as a shrimp boat for southern waters. Before completion she was laid out and equipped as a cruising boat, making a perfect floating home for Mrs. John Brooks for more than ten years. Though her home port was Southport, Connecticut, she made an annual migration down the Intracoastal Waterway to spend the winter in her native Florida waters. Several times Katy and I made the trip, enjoying the company of Bikie and our friend Tom Waddington, *Uncle Jack*'s skipper. Photograph by Norman Fortier, neg. 17576. (Courtesy of the photographer)

fect. I could commute by skiff and oars from our rented cottage a few hundred yards away. Although most of Captiva's small craft were powerboats designed to get their owners quickly to the fishing or shelling grounds, *Dixie Belle* and her sail and oars fitted our needs perfectly.

For some ten years, Katy and I spent part of each spring and fall as guests of Bikie (Mrs. John) Brooks aboard her 65-foot modified shrimper *Uncle Jack*. We had met Bikie through Drayton Cochran. She lived aboard the vessel in Southport, Connecticut, during the summer and sailed aboard her out of Palm Beach during the winter. For the trip down and back through the Intercoastal Waterway, Bikie employed our friend and hers, Tom Waddington, as captain. She invited Katy and me to come along as kitchen helper and deckhand. As Bikie planned it, we cruised along slowly, stopping at specified places of interest. Tom knew the waterway well, having made the trip often during the war and at other times on private yachts. He was a fine navigator and a superb boat-handler. To get a 65-footer with a single screw and no bow-thruster into an 80-foot slot in a crowded marina takes real skill and knowledge of docklines.

Comfort and ease we had aplenty. Bikie had a big stateroom aft: Katy and I had a fine one amidships; and Tom had good, airy quarters forward. With a big cockpit that we called our back porch, two big above-deck day cabins–living rooms, really–and a galley and dining area forward, we were cruising first-class, for sure. Although she was not fast, *Uncle Jack* had an easy motion underway. At anchor she set a steadying sail aft on the housetop. Although the sail was small (it was actually an old tan-barked staysail from *Integrity*), it kept the boat's head to wind at anchor and greatly reduced rolling at all times. In all, *Uncle Jack* was a perfect example of a workboat successfully converted for pleasure.

Ralph Wiley designed and built the 48-foot shoal-draft motorsailer *Wanderer*, launching her in 1940. When my friend Dick Borden was looking for a boat to use in the Bahamas for photographing birds and fish, I checked with Pete Culler and he suggested I contact Ralph Wiley. During a delightful visit to his Oxford, Maryland, boatyard I was introduced to the Chesapeake style of motorsailer and found *Wanderer* to be just the able, livable, easily handled shoal-draft boat to suit Dick Borden's needs. He bought her, and Pete Culler helped me engage Art Hansen as skipper for Dick. As Katy and I learned during two winter cruises, *Wanderer* was a wonderful cruising boat, especially with Art Hansen as captain, navigator, engineer, tour guide, and assistant cook. She was photographed in the Bahamas in 1959. Unidentified photographer. (Author's collection)

And I must mention one other yacht that enhanced my appreciation of the virtues of a traditional workboat type. This was the 48-foot shoal-draft motorsailer *Wanderer*, built in Oxford, Maryland, to designs by Ralph Wiley, on which Katy and I made two winter cruises in the Bahamas. *Wanderer* had many of the characteristics of the cross-planked vee-bottom Chesapeake boats. She was a wonderful cruiser, and she had the added virtue of being commanded by Art Hanson. Right after World War II, Art had bought a beautiful piece of property, "Sea to Sea," on Abaco Island, for which he paid ten dollars. Aboard his little ketch *Jolly Tar*, Art sailed to Falmouth, Massachusetts, in the spring and back to the Bahamas for the winter. *Jolly Tar* had many of the characteristics of a Bahamian sloop.

I mention *Wanderer*, *Jolly Tar*, and *Uncle Jack* to emphasize the great number of time-tested traditional workboats that have been adapted for pleasure use, and why it is so important for Mystic Seaport to have information on surviving examples of such old-timers for Museum visitors seeking guidance in making their own choice of cruising boats.

Art Hansen's 36-foot ketch, *Jolly Tar*, was designed by Fenwick Williams and incorporated elements of the Bahamian sloops. Here she is off T Wharf, Boston, where Hansen lived as a photographer in Boston. Later she carried him between his homes on Abaco in the Bahamas and Falmouth on Cape Cod. When Coast Guard regulations reduced the number of charter passengers Hansen could carry, he put his knowledge of Bahamian waters to use as skipper of Dick Borden's *Wanderer*. Reliable and companionable, an experienced sailor and a conscientious boat keeper, Art had all the attributes of a first-class skipper. (Mystic Seaport 1995.84.167)

Now, some rude awakenings.

In the late 1980s I basked in the assurance that, aside from the usual growing pains that plague every organization and individual, Mystic Seaport was sailing along in good shape. It had the best of locations, many fine and unique exhibits well displayed, and a reliable means of maintaining its fleet. Especially in the educational field, where many new activities were underway, the Museum had a breadth and quality that promised to hold it in the forefront among maritime museums.

As I got older it became difficult for me to get to the Museum as often as I wished to, but I did continue to attend the fall trustee meetings and I did say my piece whenever I felt I had a constructive idea to offer. Then, almost overnight, conditions changed unexpectedly for me and understandably for Mystic Seaport. First, I suddenly lost a great deal of my eyesight. I could no longer drive a car or read and write in the usual way. Then my enthusiasm for constructive activities deserted me, because of a mostly unrecognized malady that the doctors were learning to call depression.

The hardest blow came for me in 1991, when my dear wife, Katy, died of cancer. This left me in the doldrums from which I escaped only when I came to realize that I had already had as long and as lovely a married life as anyone could possibly expect to enjoy. My glass, for so many months empty, slowly started to refill.

I was aroused into positive action again by reading the report of the spring 1994 meeting of Mystic Seaport's board of trustees. As I understood the report, the Museum had been promised funds by the State of Connecticut with which to enhance the Museum and thus encourage more tourism in that area of Connecticut. There would, of course, be limiting restrictions on how the Museum might use the money–and would be accountable to the state for it. Rereading the report, I began to feel that the board and administration might be in danger of compromising the basic values of the Seaport. I therefore decided to take the summer off from working on this book and to express my concerns and hopes as loudly and widely as I could.

Basically, I found the Museum's current situation much like that of 40 years before, when visitor attendance had started to slow down and annual expenses had grown faster than the income to cover them. Now as then, it seemed to me that Mystic Seaport was trying to cure the problem by promoting entertainment at the expense of historical enlightenment. I did understand that income must keep pace with expenses. I also knew that the Museum had been developing new projects of vital importance that required additional income. And I knew that Mystic Seaport was not alone in experiencing a fall-off in public attendance. Something had to be done. The question was what?

Here is where I parted company with some members of the board and the administration of Mystic. In my view, various trustees and staffers did not fully understand or appreciate Mystic Seaport's unique and most important assets: its location, its ships and watercraft collection, and its authentic seaport setting and amenities. Instead of seeking to improve and promote these assets, a move was afoot to create something entirely new and spectacular–such as a big, glamorous, high-tech exhibition building to be sited at the Museum between Greenmanville Avenue and the waterfront. Rightly or wrongly, I believed that this would be a serious and, in the end, costly mistake. Such a structure would, I felt, confuse, if not destroy the aura of a living seaport that we had all worked so long to create. It would necessarily add to our maintenance and staffing costs, even if construction cost of the building itself was covered by the state. I felt that we already had more good static exhibits than a visitor could take in during one visit. I doubted that the project would add appreciably to our gate income for any length of time, even in the traditionally slow winter months.

As always, trustees and staff had other important concerns to discuss and decide on at their next meeting. Even more than usual, my own focus was on the waterfront and maritime exhibits. So, in an attempt reach the Trustees and staff, I first thought in terms of a written statement that might discuss, say, the desirability of installing a solid gold, jewel-studded bathtub in your own living room.

This I thought might be a real grabber. For a bathtub, no matter how beautiful, would surely change the ambience of any living room. Before embarking on this line of persuasion, however, I fortunately remembered Clifford Ashley's admonition to me of many years before. "Never be as funny as you can be, Waldo," Clifford had said. So I changed tacks.

Because pictures are more convincing and less confrontional than many words, I put together a little leaflet that would include black-and-white sketches to make my points more clearly. The front page included a simple chart of the waterfront basin, which, strangely enough, few Mystic Seaport Trustees had ever seen or studied. I titled the leaflet *The River The River The River.*

Having no ready sketch of Mystic Seaport to use in making my point, and

The author and his daughter Susie contemplate the Mystic River and the *Charles W. Morgan* from Chubb's Wharf, 1986. Photograph by Howard Means. (Courtesy of Susie Means)

also to avoid confusing the issue, I chose to adapt a drawing that Lois Darling had made for me years before and that I had reproduced in the first volume of *A Life In Boats.* First, I reproduced the drawing as Lois had created it: a peaceful, harmonious harbor scene, where each pictorial element contributes to the balance and appeal of the whole. Then I asked artist and photographer Norman Fortier to alter it in five different ways, to suggest how easy it is to spoil a good picture–or a wonderful seaport.

As the leaflet evolved, I sent copies first to top Mystic Seaport staffers to get their views on my thinking and suggestions. Then I sent copies in whole or part to particular friends of mine on the board, most of whom were members of one or more Museum committees. Finally, I discussed my ideas in great detail with the subcommittee of the Ships Committee.

By and large, reactions to *The River The River The River* were favorable. Some said that they had just taken the waterfront for granted and hadn't realized quite how special and wonderful it was. Others said that henceforth they would look at the Museum's waterfront in a new way. To what extent these responses were heartfelt or sincere, or merely polite or dutiful, I will not presume to judge. I also accept the fact that other viewpoints than mine have value and consequence and deserve to be considered and debated–and doubtless will be for as long as Mystic Seaport exists. But I am glad I spoke up. I hope others who share my love of Mystic Seaport will continue to speak up long after I am gone.

Surely by this time my readers will have gathered that the prevailing winds of my life have blown delightfully fair and that I have thoroughly enjoyed them all. I have come to the realizations that no thoughts of big business for big money have ever arisen to confuse my own compass course. Rather it has been my privilege and good fortune to follow a seemingly ordained avocation in boating. I do not mean to suggest that the avocation has been free of hard work and fixed determination, but I can avow with sincerity and satisfaction that priceless dividends have constantly come my way in the form of a wonderful wife and family and a most rewarding consistent association with the finest people and best of boats. As most working folks grow older they seem to reach a stage where retirement becomes a controlling factor, and a resulting change in daily life occurs. Not so, however, for the likes of me, who has been happily immersed in an absorbing occupation. The same old enthusiasms, modified perhaps by necessity, just keep arolling along, much like the Old Man River.

Index

Index
(Index includes both text and captions. Boldface numerals indicate illustrations.)

A
Aldrich, Dick and Daisy, 88, 96
Alerion (sloop), 171
Allyn, Robert, 134, 142, **143**, 150, 157, 166
America's Cup races, 90, 98
Anderson, Charlie, **158**
Annie (sloop), 171
Antigua, 102
Antique and Classic Boat Rendezvous (Mystic Seaport), 173
Antilles (ketch), 90
Archer, Jimmy, **72**
Ashley, Clifford W., 21, 184
Astral (bark), 32

B
Baddeck, Nova Scotia, 97
Bahamian fishing sloops, **172**, 173
Ballast keel, 54
Bandsaw, 52, 135, **136**
Baron, Maurice, **135**
Bartram, J. Burr, 98, 115
Bates, Al, 129
Baudro, Gene, 124, **135**
Beetle Cat, 26, 29, 49
Bemis, Alan, 108, 109
Bird of Passage (motorsailer), 179
Bogue, Calvin, 128, **136**, 167, **168**
Borden, Dick, 181, 182
Borden, Mrs. Spencer, 175
Bow, Clara, 16
Bray Maynard, **123**, 124, 126, 129, 150, 151, 158, 159
Brooks, Bikie (Mrs. John), 44, 180
Bulkheads (Mystic Seaport), **164**, 165, 166, **167**, **168**, 169
Burns, Terry, 98

C
Calabretta, Fred, 177
Camden, Maine, 97
Captiva Island, Florida, 179-80
Carr, J. Revell, 163, 169, **176**
Charles W. Morgan (whaleship), **14-15, 16,** 17, **114**, 115, **119**, 120, 124, **138**, 139, **142**, **143**, **144**, **145**, **146**, **153**, **154**, **155**, 157, **159**, **160-61**
Childs, Barbara, 132
Chubb, Corinne Alsop, 132, **151**, 179
Chubb, Hendon, 151
Chubb, Percy II, 90, 98, 131-32, 150, **151**, **153**, 163, 179
Chubb's Wharf (Mystic Seaport), 150-51, **152-53**
Cochran, Drayton, 91, 109, 163, 180
Concordia Sloop Boat, **31**
Concordia 31 (sloop), 29, **34**, 134
Conley, Alonzo R., 45, 46
Crocker, Sam, 35
Cruising Club of America, 91-**93,** 95, 96-97, 103, 107, 177
Culler, Robert D. (Pete), 44, **45**, 46-48, 50, 86, **87**, 91-94, 100, 118, **122**, 181
Culler, Toni, 44, 91
Cyane (sloop), 97

D
Darling, Lois, 184
d'Estang, Nancy, 159
De Grass, Caes, 105, **106**
Defiance (schooner), **46**, 47, **86**
Dixie Belle, (sailing skiff), **178**, 179
Dock, 148
Dolan, Rose, 47
Douglas, Robert, 95
Down to the Sea in Ships, 16
duPont, Henry B. and Emily, 97, 124

E
Electric Boat division of General Dynamics, 167
Emery, George, **159**, 163

Emery, Jim, 163
Escape (cutter), 17-18, 25

F
Fastenings, 54-55
Fetcher (powerboat), 47, 98
"Flattie" tender, 36, **37**
Flying Cloud II (schooner), 28, 175, 176
Fortier, Norman, 184
Foster, Anthony (Chuck), 105, **106**
Foto (powerboat), **174**
Frenning, Blanche Borden, 172

G
Galena (cutter), **120**
George and Susan (whaleship), 12, **13**
Giblin, James L., 159, 169
Gifford, Wilton, 18-20, 24-25
Gillette, Robert, 151-52
Girl Scout Mariners, 96, 103
Glory Anna II (Block Island boat), 141
Gowen & Company, 75
Green, Edward Howland Robinson, 11, 14, 17, 162
Greenheart, 54
Grinnell, Arthur, 13

H
Hackmatack, **134**-35
Half model, 50
Hambidge, Roger, **157**
Hammond, Paul, **89**, 90, 172
Hammond, Suzie, 90
Hanson, Art, 181-82
Hardy, Harold E., **78**, 79-81, 94-95
Harris, Wilder B. (Bill), 29
Henry B. duPont Preservation Shipyard (Mystic Seaport), 124, **125**, 126, **127**, **128**, 129, 156-57
Herreshoff 12 1/2 (sloop), **170**, 171
Herreshoff 16 footer, 171
Herrington, Arthur W., 79-**80**, 88, 91, 94-95, 96-97, 103, 104-05, **106**, 107, 108, 110-11, 172
Hewson, Dana, 159
Holbrook, Robert, 152
Howland, Barnabas, 11
Howland, Charlie, 91, 94, 103, 104, **106**
Howland, George, 24
Howland, Gideon, 11
Howland, Hope Waldo, 5, 19
Howland, Katherine (Katy), **18**, 44, **78**, 81, 85, **100**, 103, 171, 179, 180, 181, 182
Howland, Kinnaird, **31**, **41**, 79, 81, 84, 85, **87**, 91, 94, 95, 96, 98, **102**, 103, 104, 105, **106**
Howland, Priscilla, 16
Howland, Susie (Mrs. Howard Means), **31**, 103, **184**
Howland, Tom, **73**, 79, **81**, 85, 94, **100**, **102**, 103
Howland, Waldo, **18**, **63**, **64**, **65**, **88**, **122**, **164**, **173**, **176**, **178**, **184**
Howland, Waldo Jr., **102**, 103, 115
Howland house (Round Hill), **10**
Howland house (55 High Street), 11, **12**, 13
Howland house (author's home), 18, **19**, **20**, **21**, **22**, 23-25
Hurricane Carol, 47
Hurricane Hugo, 133

I
Ingomar (schooner), **175**, 176
Integrity (schooner), **9**, 27-28, **42**, **86**, **101**, **110**; design of, **47**-48, 50-**51**; construction of, **53**, **55-67**; launch of, **68-69**; rig of, **70-71**, **73**, **74**, **82-83**; engine of, **72**, 87; benefits of, 72-75; sails of, 75, **76**, **77**, **84**; ballast added, 87; sailing in Caribbean, 99, 101; transatlantic passage, 106, 107, **108**; loss of 111
Intrepid (sloop), 98

J
Jackson, Martin, 21, **44**, 118
Jag (spritsail boat), 31-32
Jarvis, Henry, 143, **158**
Java (beach boat), **34**, **78**
Java II (beach boat), **100**, 101
Johnston, Waldo C.M., 115, 116-17, 119, 123, **145**, 176
Jointer, 52
Jolly Tar (ketch), 181-**82**
Joseph Conrad (ship), 120

K
Kingston II (tugboat), 167
Kneedler, Franklin, 163, 169

L
Lampson, Robert, 98
Landfall (ketch), 172
Larr, Timothea, 176, 177
Leavitt, John F., **117**, 118, 123
Lexia (cutter), 175, 176
Lift dock, **128**-29
Live oak (see Oak)
Locust, 20-22, **133**, 134

Luke, Paul 47
Lynch, Edward, 123

M
Mallory, Clifford and Pauline, **121**, 122, 124, 163
Mallory shipyard, **113**, 124
Manchester Yacht Sails, 75
Mary Ellen (sloop), **34**
Mayo, Charlie, 44-45
Melbourne, Florida, 35, 36
Menemsha Pond (Martha's Vineyard), Massachusetts, 33, **40-41**
Molloy, Bill, 144
Muskrat (powerboat), 36-37, **38**
Muskrat II (powerboat design), **39**
Mystic River, Connecticut, 115-16, 184-85
Mystic Seaport, 90, 115, 117-18, **120**, **125**, 183-85
"Mystic way," 128, 159, 153, 166, 167, 168-69

N
Neel, Leon, 132
New Bedford Yacht Club, 43, 81
New York Yacht Club, 81, 89, 95
Newport 29 (sloop), 171
Neyland, Harry, 17
Nielsen, Aage, 47
Nonquitt (South Dartmouth), Massachusetts, 30

O
Oak, 53-54; live, **133**, **157** white, 133-34
Ogden, Alfred, **121**,
Olad II (schooner), **44**
Owens Yacht Corporation, 135

P
Parkinson, John Jr., 81, 90, 109, 115
Pearson, Jeff, **135**, **159**
Pellegrina (yawl), 47
Peterson, Murray, 48
Pier, 148
Pierce, Elmer, 20, 22, 23, 25
Pierce, Mark, 95, 96, 98, **100**, 105, **106**, 109
Pine, white, 23-24, 54, 70, **130**, 134; yellow, 54, 131-**32**
Plant, Morton, 175
Ponte, Charlie, 20
Porkess, Jill, **104**, 105, **106**
Prospector, (ketch), **29**
Punt, 31

R
Rachel B. Jackson (schooner), **163**
Randall, Leslie, **67**
Rara Avis (Thames River barge), **89**, 90
Regina M. (sardine carrier), 137
Resolute (launch), 90
Rigadoon (schooner), 47
Rigg, Linton (Bunny), 103, 172
River The River The River, The, 184-85
Robinson, Donald, 122, 123, 150, **158**, 159, 166, 167
Rogers, Francis Day, 119
Rosenfeld, Morris, **174**
Rosenfeld, Stanley, **174**-76
Rosenfeld Collection (Mystic Seaport), 173-76
Rotch, Sarah, 30
Round Hill (South Dartmouth), Massachusetts, **10, 14, 15,** 17
Rousseau (whaleship), 13
Royal Cork Yacht Club, 104, 107
Royal Cruising Club, 107

S
St. John, New Brunswick, 92
Sankaty (steamer), 16
Sawmill (Mystic Seaport), **135**
Scheel, Henry, 119, 122
Sea Breeze (sloop), 43
Seawanhaka Corinthian Yacht Club, 177
Shenandoah (schooner), **95**
Shepler, Dwight, 109
Shipbuilding tools, 52
Ships Committee (Mystic Seaport), 119-23, 143, 145, 185
Shipsaw (see Bandsaw)
Smyth, Major William, **119**, 122, **123**
Snediker, Quentin, 133, 159
Snow, Viv, 98
Soil Conservation Service, 168
Spar lathe, 135-**36**
Special Demonstrations Squad (Mystic Seaport), 139-**40**
Spray (yawl), 44, 45, 46
Star Class, 177
Stephens, Olin J. II, 123, 177
Stetson, Bill and Katie, 103
Strongman, Louise, 96
Swift, Rodman, 30-40

T
Tall Ships parade, 88
Thickness planer, 52, 135
Tilton, George Fred, 17
Tripp, Ben, 25
Tyche (schooner), **33-34**, 35, 39, **40**
Tyrell boatyard, 107

U
Uncle Jack (powerboat), 44, **180-81**
U.S. Army Corps of Engineers, 166

V
Vanda (ketch), 101, 109
Vaughn-Jones, Bob and Heddy, 101, 109

W
Waddington, Tom, 43-44, **45**, 48, 180
Walter, Jarillo (Jay), 90
Wanderer (motorsailer), **181**, 182
Weeks, Allan, 179
Welch, Charles, 94
Whaling Enshrined, 17
Wharf design, 147-**49**
White, Joel, 108-09, 159
Whitman, Nicholas, 27-28
Wiley, Ralph, 181
William P. Stephens Award (Mystic Seaport), 177
Williams, Fenwick, 39, 182
Wilson, Fred, 168
Winnie of Bourne (yawl), 81

Y
Yachting Committee (Mystic Seaport), 176-77
Yachting History Symposium (Mystic Seaport), 177
Yates, Rex, **104**, 105, **106**, 109
Yellow pine (see Pine), 54, 131-**32**

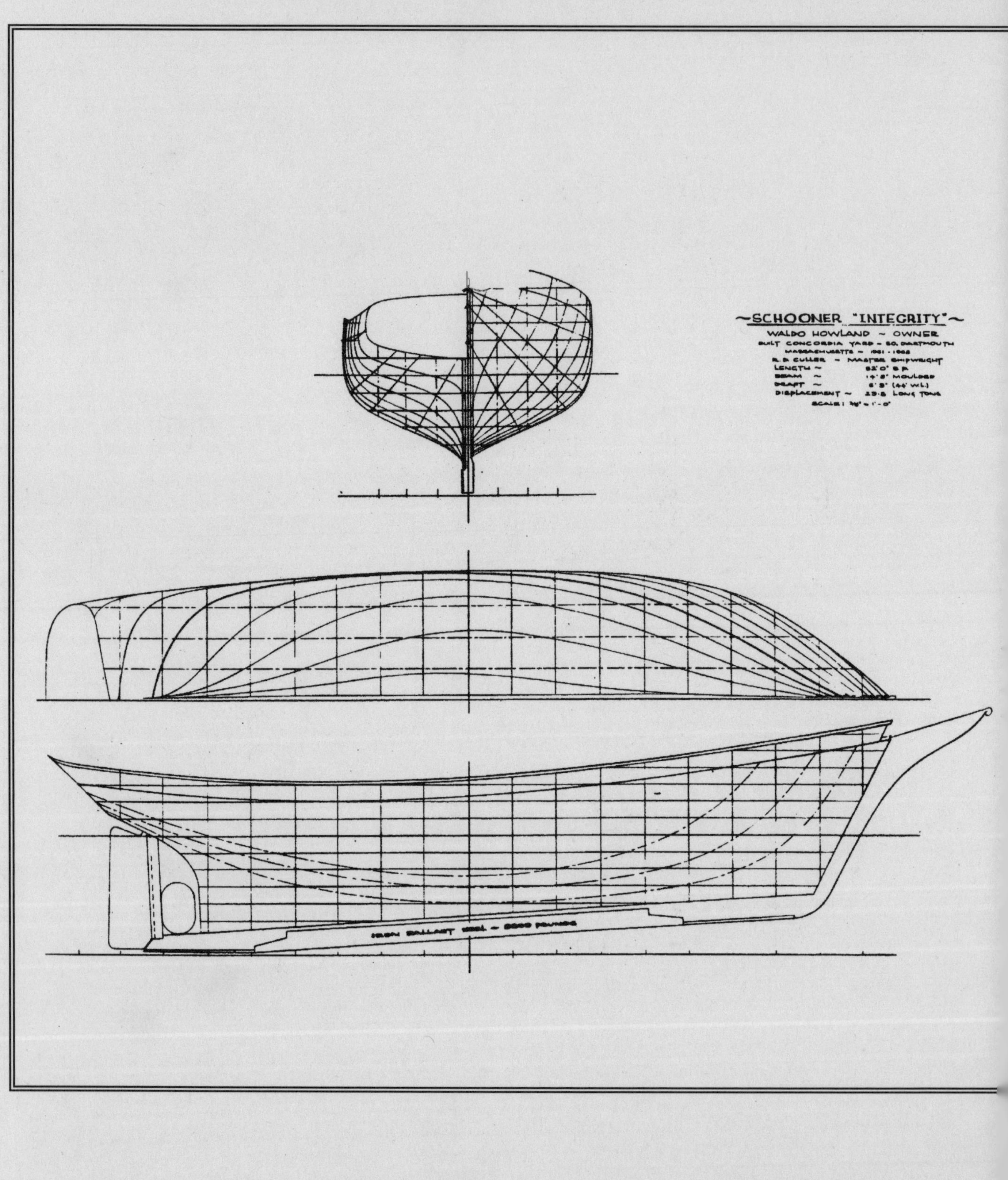
~SCHOONER "INTEGRITY"~
WALDO HOWLAND ~ OWNER
BUILT CONCORDIA YARD – SO. DARTMOUTH
MASSACHUSETTS
R. D. CULLER – MASTER SHIPWRIGHT
LENGTH ~
BEAM ~ 14' 8" MOULDED
DRAFT ~ (44' W.L.)
DISPLACEMENT ~ LONG TONS
IRON BALLAST KEEL – POUNDS